INDEX

HEALTHY MEDITERRANEAN COOKING

HEALTHY MEDITERRANEAN COOKING

RENA SALAMAN

PHOTOGRAPHS BY GUS FILGATE

SERIES EDITOR
LEWIS ESSON

STEWART, TABORI & CHANG
NEW YORK

To my lovely daughters, Sophie and Alexandra

Healthy Mediterranean Cooking
Copyright © 1996 Frances Lincoln Limited
Text copyright © 1996 Rena Salaman
Photographs copyright © 1996 Frances Lincoln Limited

Published in 1996 and distributed in the United States by
Stewart, Tabori & Chang,
a division of U.S. Media Holdings, Inc.
575 Broadway, New York, N.Y. 10012

Distributed in Canada by General Publishing Co. Ltd.
30 Lesmill Road, Don Mills, Ontario
Canada M3B 2T6

Library of Congress Catalog Card Number:
96–69739
ISBN 1-55670-498-4

Designed by Frances Lincoln Limited

Printed and bound in Hong Kong by Paramount Printing Co. Ltd.
10 9 8 7 6 5 4 3 2 1
First Edition

NUTRITIONAL INFORMATION

The figures given in the nutritional information panel that accompanies each recipe are per serving and have been rounded off to the nearest whole number. Optional ingredients and variations have not been included in the calculations and the figures are based on the largest number of suggested servings.

The ranges given for fat, protein and carbohydrate content are based on the proportion each makes of total calorie content as follows.
Total fat: Low = under 20%; Medium = 20-33%; High = over 33%
Saturated fat: Low = under 5%; Medium = 5-10%; High = over 10%
Protein: Low = under 15%; Medium = 15-20%; High = over 20%
Carbohydrate: Low = under 50%; Medium = 50-60%; High = over 60%
The cholesterol rating "none" also covers negligible trace amounts.

Please note that such a system can occasionally produce results that seem surprising when not viewed in a wider context. For example, a salad dressed with only 2 tablespoons of oil can have a very low overall calorie count, so its fat content then reads as "high" in this system. However, were that salad to be analyzed together with just one accompanying slice of bread the increase in total calories could reduce the level of fat to "medium" or even "low."

Throughout the book the olive oil content of dishes has been reduced from traditional generous amounts and, if you are attempting to curb fat intake, you may lower them even further. However, its use has been kept at an optimum level to achieve authentic flavors and to ensure the benefits of olive oil's health-giving properties when consumed in moderation.

CONTENTS

A MEDITERRANEAN JOURNEY

Romantics and simple travelers alike have eulogized the Mediterranean through the centuries. Shelley in his "Ode to the West Wind" sang about its blue waters, Goethe spoke of "the land where the lemon trees blossom" and Norman Douglas in *Siren Land* urged his readers to "mediterraneanize" themselves, even if only for a season.

As I sit under the shade of the big glossy-leaved mulberry tree in our garden on an Aegean island and gaze at the blue expanse beyond the hills where the sea quietly joins the horizon, I feel the full impact of all those other travelers. There it all is…The lemon trees (admittedly not flowering, as it is late July), the almond trees loaded with heavy fruit, the fig trees with their erotic smell under the midday sun, and of course the queen of all—the olive tree. Could we perceive the Mediterranean without the olive tree?

Then the different characters start to parade as if out of a play. First morning visitor is Stavros, who collects garbage with his mule during the summer, but who is passionate about and an expert on trees. He sips his tiny cup of Greek coffee and gives an appraisal on our trees. The mulberry will have to be pruned severely if we are to limit its production of huge white sugary fruit that attracts the wasps in thousands earlier in July. (I would have risked my life sitting under it two weeks ago.) The vines will need some manure if the grapes are to be improved, and the almond trees are getting straggly. But on another note, did we hear about the extraordinary amounts of squid that Nikos the carpenter had caught last night? Yes, we later did as a bag full of wonderful squid arrived as a present from Nikos, distributing some of his excessive catch after complaints from his good wife that she has run out of space in the refrigerator.

Stavros's wife Nina runs the family *taverna* in one of the cobbled streets at the heart of the village. Stavros mentions that our favorite *yiouvetsi*—a dish of goat or lamb and pasta with fresh tomatoes and quantities of garlic—is on the menu tonight as Tassos the shepherd has slaughtered a couple of his goats. How could we miss that? Tassos's goats roam the hills around the village, as their bells announce them daily, and they feed on the purple flowers of the thyme that covers the hillsides. Sometimes they also feed on people's plants over the garden walls and then they are not popular at all. As for Nina's intimacy with a first-class *yiouvetsi*, we are well aware of that.

Next the tiny, bird-like but agile Penelope—her woollen socks drooping round her ankles and her badly worn, ruby-studded black patent leather shoes, a couple of sizes too large for her tiny feet—almost hops over the garden wall, with her apron gathered. Some fresh eggs from her hens are nestling in there. They will make a perfect omelet, cooked with some sweet tomatoes at lunchtime.

And then arrives old bony one-toothed Barba Nikos with his hawk-like nose and a leathered skin like a lizard's, who builds the lace-like stone walls around our gardens. He brings golden apricots from his trees and bunches of *rigani*—oregano—and gives us the latest village gossip while sipping a cold beer. He recounts his early morning outing with his friend from Athens, Stratigos, "the General," in search of *pikrohorto*, a frightfully bitter herb which, when taken as a tisane, lowers the blood pressure and makes you immortal like the gods, according to Nikos. Having tried it a few years ago, I can still feel my teeth numb

with the excessive bitterness. Did Socrates feel the same way drinking his *conium,* I wondered.

These are the different puzzle pieces that constitute the Mediterranean. The people, the distinctive trees, the aromatic hillsides, the sea—with all its bounty—and the delicious food that has been born out of the combinations of all these. Following the food trail around the Mediterranean is like following the people. Although each country has its distinctive signature in the kitchen, the same primary ingredients play first violin and so a number of similar dishes are to be found around this fabled sea: the seasonal vegetables quickly fried or grilled and served with fresh soured or grilled cheeses or garlicky sauces, or occasionally pulped into savory dips, the fish and the seafood, the salads which appear in unusual combinations with fruit and nuts and the winter soups made with beans, chickpeas and lentils.

There are also those unmistakable underlying links which are olive oil and the herbs that enhance the dishes. The links are also seen in the way the dishes are served and in the spirit in which they are consumed, as life revolves and evolves round the table in the Mediterranean.

Finally to the poets and travelers past and present eulogizing about the Mediterranean, most recently doctors and dieticians have added their voices—this time about the Mediterranean diet and not any more just about its tastes and colors, but about its healthiness. The grains, legumes, fresh fruit and vegetables, the high-protein fish, lean meat and poultry, the olive oil and wine that are its staples are now recognized as providing the ultimate healthy diet. Low in cholesterol and saturated fats and high in fiber and vitamins, it also supplies an abundance of the protective agents that are thought to actively combat disease and enhance life expectancy.

THE HEALTHY MEDITERRANEAN DIET

What exactly is this healthy Mediterranean diet? To me, this diet recently appraised as healthy was what I was brought up on—the seasonal vegetables cooked with lots of garlic and onions and brought alive with lemons or tomatoes, the bean and lentil soups in the winter, the cheese pies, the abundant fruit, and fresh salads with every meal. This was what we and our friends and neighbors ate daily, and we did not seem to have weight problems, cardiovascular disorders, or too many other ailments.

Of course the main protagonist of the cooking pot, as well as the table, is the aromatic fruity green olive oil which, among fats, is the richest source of the desirable monounsaturated fatty acids contained in its large amounts of oleic acid (see page 10).

The original research project on the subject was carried out by the United Nations on Crete in the 1950s, prompted by the history of longevity on the island, as well as the absence of cardiovascular disease. However, we knew nothing of this research or its convincing results. Olive oil was simply embedded at the root of our lives. We did not know butter, as it virtually did not exist—even now I don't use it and I don't miss it. As for meat, it was served in small quantities on Sundays and then more often as ground meat in stuffed vegetables or in meat rissoles.

Instead, we had fish and seafood of all kinds. Everyone knew that fish was lean and healthy, containing a number of nutrients and vitamins. Our grandmothers had a standard phrase for seafood: "Good for the eyes [containing phosphorus], the blood [it lowers cholesterol] and the brain [vitamin E]." Modern research has proved that it is the omega-3 fatty acids contained in fish oil that have all these beneficial qualities. So, squid, cuttlefish, mussels and occasionally razor clams were made into *pilafs* or fried to accompany the lentil soups or bean salads. Slim elongated silver anchovies sprinkled with garlic, fresh tomatoes and olive oil or small whole tuna dotted with garlic and wrapped in paper were sent to the ovens at the local bakers. Fish soups were assembled with a variety of different small bony fish called *petropsara*—rockfish—and the occasional eel. Salt cod was treated in a multitude of ways and a small piece of it would go a long way. The diet was a combination of frugality and tradition. The latter being itself born out of frugality anyway.

The abundance of vegetables and legumes—with their many nutrients, their vitamins, minerals and fiber—made up the main character of the Mediterranean diet. And olive oil was, on the whole, what gave flavor to the dishes. Admittedly it was quite often used in large quantities. However olive oil, as we have seen, has been proved beneficial to health. So the Mediterranean diet is healthy in its very nature. With a few adjustments it can become even more so.

Writing this book has been a natural outcome of the recognition of the diet's healthiness. Nevertheless, in an effort to make the recipes even healthier, if that is possible, I have lowered the amounts of olive oil used—although not too drastically, so its flavor is still prevalent. If you are counting calories you can lower the amount of olive oil (and nuts) even further.

Throughout the book, however, the focus is on vegetables, legumes and seafood. Butter and cream have been kept to a minimum and may be omitted altogether. Cheese, particularly in Italian cooking, is so indispensable that it would have seemed unnatural to eliminate it altogether. Anyway, cheeses like Parmesan have such a powerful flavor that only very little is needed. There are, however, other important factors in the Mediterranean diet's healthy character; that is, how a meal is assembled and consumed.

MEDITERRANEAN MEALS

The Mediterranean *mezze* approach to a meal concentrates on variety. I prefer it not only because of its appeal to the palate but also because of its lighter character. It also inevitably slows the meal down, which is a good thing in itself.

For instance, for a fairly lavish meal with friends I serve two or three small courses, some cold and others hot, one after the other so that their flavors can be fully experienced. These may be Melitzanosalata (page 43), Tyropitakia (page 49) and Tabbouleh (page 145) or Roast Zucchini with Salsa Verde (page 44) and Puy Lentils with Dill, Salsa Verde and Roast Peppers (page 128). Then we may have a salad and after that have a main course in the form of an Asparagus Risotto (page 72) or fish, for instance. The *mezze* obviously can be as varied and elaborate as the situation dictates, or it can be simple and frugal.

For our family meals at home in Athens we would always have a large crusty loaf of fresh bread on the table. Additionally, there were bowls of olives and plates of greenery, such as arugula and little radishes or scallions and cucumbers. People would help themselves to all these throughout the meal. By stopping and introducing a new flavor, people slow down, which is healthy in itself, but also the total quantity consumed diminishes. So not only the meal itself was healthy, but so was the way it was eaten.

When planning a meal, try to add variety. Try to make the combinations well-balanced and interesting. Invite some friends and try cooking some of the dishes suggested in this book, serving them in the Mediterranean fashion. Then just sit back and observe the results. At least liveliness—if not intoxication—will be hovering in the air.

Rena Salaman, Summer 1995

SOME MEDITERRANEAN INGREDIENTS

"Let food be your medicine" said the father of medicine, Hippocrates (460-337 BC).

OLIVE OIL AND OLIVES

If there was one tree with which to identify the Mediterranean, it would be the olive tree, *Olea europaea*, which has grown wild in the area since time immemorial. I have seen wild gnarled olive trees being grafted and have experienced their miraculous conversion once they start to sprout tame branches with bigger leaves. Weather-beaten, water-starved and scorched by the strong summer sun, they still manage to produce their wondrous fruit.

The olive tree, with its beautiful silver leaves, has been the source of the most important ingredient in the Mediterranean kitchen, olive oil, and another important ingredient on the table, the olive itself. According to historical sources, both of these were used abundantly in ancient Greece and it was the ancient seafaring Greeks who brought the olive tree west as far as Spain and Provence.

Fresh olives off the tree are inedible as they are incredibly bitter. Take a tiny bite off one and your mouth will be completely numb. So it is a marvel that this inedible fruit can be transformed in such a way by the time it reaches the table. This is done by cracking or slicing the olives and immersing them in cold water, which has to be changed daily for at least ten to fifteen days. Once through this process, they lose their bitterness and they can then be salted and flavored with added aromatics and spices.

When the olives are picked from the tree while still unripe and green, which happens in early September, they are treated for their bitterness and they are then our familiar green olives, which have a refreshing taste and harder texture. Once the olives have turned dark violet-blue or black on the tree—which starts to happen around the middle of October—then these black olives have a more complex flavor than the green ones. However, black olives can be tricky, as I have found by experience. Occasionally, after we have soaked them in water to extract their bitterness they can become completely tasteless and bland. It is at that stage that we marinate them with salt, garlic cloves, bay leaves, coriander seeds, chilies and anything else that takes our fancy.

Olives ripen earlier or later according to the position of the trees, the soil and the weather. For the purposes of olive oil, they have to be picked at a medium stage, when they are still hard and on the tree, before they shrivel and fall off. Green unripe olives produce a small yield of olive oil, which also contains a lower quantity of oleic acid. As the olives ripen they produce more oil, with a higher yield of oleic acid. Oleic acid is the factor that determines their classification. "Extra-virgin oil" must contain less than 1% oleic acid, in fact the cognoscenti believe that it should not be more than 0.5%. Olive oil with a higher acidity of anything between 1.5 and 3 is generally classified as "virgin." Acidity, however, is not the only criterion. Extra-virgin olive oil must also meet high standards of flavor, aroma and color.

Olives are labor-intensive, because they have to be picked by hand, as any mechanical process might bruise them. Once harvested, olives have to be transported to the olive mill as soon as possible before they start to ferment as their acidity level increases. There they are washed mechanically in cold water and the leaves and small branches are separated from the fruit automatically. They are then crushed

and mixed with water. The oil, once separated from the water in a centrifuge, drips into vats. Generally today any oil from this first mechanical pressing (as opposed to later chemical extraction) is claimed to be from the "first cold pressing" (a term not defined by international agreement). So one must not pay too much heed to such a description. The main factors in flavor are olive variety, and local soil and climate, etc.

Olive oil has a great diversity in taste. It can be golden, sweet and smooth—as is French olive oil often—or dark green with a strong fruity taste like Greek olive oil. This is a matter of personal choice and it frequently means that one can use different oils for different occasions and dishes. Throughout this book I have not specified extra-virgin oil because I assume that one would not want to use anything else.

Olive oil does not keep forever and it has to be stored in a dark and cool place. In my experience on Alonnisos, where the oil is stored in large *pytharia,* it holds its taste for about two years, and after that it may go rancid, developing an unmistakable and

unpleasant "engine oil" taste and smell.

Recently a lot has been written about olive oil and its beneficial effects on our health. Basically olive oil contains no cholesterol and it is a monounsaturated fat, which contains a large concentration of Vitamin E and HDLs (high-density lipoproteins). HDLs lower cholesterol in the system and also act against the harmful LDLs (low-density lipoproteins), which in turn accumulate cholesterol and deposit it on the arterial walls. Olive oil not only contains these valuable HDLs but also—unlike other oils—it does not destroy the body's own natural resources of these HDLs. Polyunsaturated oils like the vegetable oils, on the other hand, while they lower the harmful LDLs also deplete the body's own beneficial HDLs.

VEGETABLES
Vegetables are a natural source of all kinds of nutrients, such as proteins as well as vitamins, minerals, fiber and antioxidants, these last being vigorous anti-cancer agents.

ARTICHOKES
The globe artichoke is for me the queen of vegetables. It can be eaten raw, when its heart is sliced thinly into salads, or cooked in casseroles or omelets or stuffed. Artichokes also signify spring, since they start to appear in the markets in March. Historically the artichoke, which is a cultivated variety of the cardoon, was developed in fifteenth-century Italy and soon spread to Greece and other Mediterranean countries.

Before use, the inedible hairy choke lying just above the heart needs to be removed. However, very young artichokes sometimes have little or no developed choke and may be cooked and eaten whole. The artichoke discolors readily, so it needs to be immersed in acidulated water or brushed with lemon juice after preparation. Artichokes are a good source of Vitamin A, folate, potassium and calcium.

ARUGULA

The bright green serrated leaves of arugula, with their strong almost spicy taste and peppery finish, are indispensable in a mixed salad. They are loved all over the Mediterranean, particularly in Italy (the Italians gave us their name), in Greece (*roka*) and in Turkey. Arugula grows like a weed, but it quickly goes to seed and the leaves should be harvested young.

Traditionally it was harvested growing wild like dandelions. The younger leaves have a milder taste and a lovely texture and can be made into a salad by themselves, perhaps with shavings of Parmesan on top as served in Italy. Alternatively, when it is older and stronger-tasting, it is better mixed with other salad greens and lettuces, including radicchio. Young leaves can be used whole, but older and coarser leaves are best first trimmed of thick stems.

The sharply appetizing taste of arugula goes well with cheese, fish and even fruit. The leaves are packed with vitamin C, B and folate.

EGGPLANTS

Although seemingly a quintessential Mediterranean vegetable, the eggplant actually came from the East, probably India. Botanically it belongs to the Solanaceae family, like the tomato, pepper and potato.

It originally tended to be bitter, so once sliced it was imperative either to immerse it in salted water for half an hour or to sprinkle the slices with salt and then rinse them. Today, with modern varieties, I find there is no bitterness, so it is not necessary to go through this any more—not with Mediterranean varieties anyway. I know that in places like India and Ceylon eggplants can still be bitter, so beware.

It is in Turkey that the love of eggplants is proverbial and they will be found there in a plethora of dishes. Eggplants are a good source of calcium, vitamin A and a smaller amount of vitamin C.

GARLIC

One wonders how Mediterranean food would have developed without garlic. This is one of the oldest and greatest flavoring ingredients, as well as being used as a medicine and in pagan rituals. It has been worshipped as a god and its strong aroma has been associated with the devil. Its original habitat may have been Western Asia and botanists believe that it came to Mesopotamia and Egypt via Asia Minor.

Garlic is rich in vitamins B and C, and in phosphorus, potassium and calcium, as well as in the antioxidant mineral selenium. It helps sugar metabolize, so it is used in the treatment of both diabetes and hypoglycemia. It aids digestion and its content of allicin, which invades the proteins in germs and destroys them, makes it also antibacterial. It also has anti-inflammatory qualities and is thus good against arthritis. Today, it is believed to lower cholesterol and to purify the blood.

The taste of garlic varies according to its age. When it is young, with firm and juicy creamy-white cloves, it has quite a sweet taste. When it has been sitting around for a while, it feels soft and papery to the touch. The cloves are a dull, yellow color, look shriveled and have a somewhat acrid taste, and should be avoided. In the spring, fresh new season's garlic can be bought. Thin and elegant, this somewhat resembles scallions and its taste is delicately fresh but unmistakable. Thinly sliced it makes a lovely addition to salads.

The best way to crush garlic is to peel it, sprinkle a little salt over it and rest the blade of a knife on it, then press to crush it and release its essential oils.

Grape Leaves

In Greece, as well as the Middle East, vine leaves are used to wrap and cook food. Stuffings made with rice, onions, herbs and nuts and with or without meat make delicious Dolmathes (see pages 126-7). Grape leaves are also used to wrap fish before baking or grilling, when they impart their aroma and lemony flavor to the dish. They are traditionally used young and fresh at the beginning of the summer.

Alternatively, they can be bought preserved in brine from Greek shops. These tend to be very salty and should be rinsed carefully first.

If you have access to fresh grape leaves you can freeze them. Rinse them first, dip them briefly in a bowl of boiling water and drain them. Pile them in groups of twenty-five, roll them up and place them in a freezer-proof container. Allow them to thaw completely for two to three hours before using them. Grape leaves contain some vitamins and a large amount of carotene and are a good source of fiber.

Okra

Okra, also known descriptively as "ladies' fingers," are the green pods of a tall annual, *Abelmoschus esculentus*, which can reach a height of six feet. The plant's green pods are covered with a light prickly skin, so the okra pickers have to wear gloves to protect their fingers against skin irritations. The pods can vary in size enormously, according to the variety. They have to be handled gently so that they do not get bruised or, worse, squashed, as this will allow their mucilaginous juices to pour out.

Okra, which originates from Africa, has a sweet taste and a pleasurable melting texture. To prepare it you have to pare the conical head lightly with a slanting movement and then trim off the black tip at the other end very slightly. (To simplify matters you can just cut the top horizontally but not too deeply.)

Okra is mostly used whole and intact in the Mediterranean, but there may be instances where it is first sliced to allow its mucilaginous substances to be incorporated in the dish, for instance in the classic New Orleans gumbo,

Okra contains a good amount of vitamin A and a smaller amount of vitamin C.

PEPPERS

Both bell peppers (*Capsicum annuum*) and chilies (*C. frutescens*) are members of the Solanaceae or nightshade family, which also includes tomatoes and potatoes. Like them, they came to Europe from the New World with Columbus in the fifteenth century. A year after his first voyage, the first seeds of *C. annuum* arrived in Spain. It was there that it established itself and got into the kitchens either roasted whole, or dried and pounded into a powder to be used instead of the black pepper which had come from India. This ground red pepper was paprika, although it did not then have the name, but instead was called West Indian pepper. This was not only a flavoring, but it also added brilliant color to sauces.

There is a bewildering array of different varieties of capsicums, probably over three hundred, with a multitude of shapes, sizes and colors. These extend from sweet bell peppers to mildly pungent and hot peppers, such as anchos, jalapeños, and the fiery hot habaneros from the West Indies. Peppers, particularly red ones, are an invaluable source of vitamins C and A. Red peppers also contain an enormous amount of beta-carotene, a valuable antioxidant.

Paprika
This red powder, made from a ground dried variety of bell pepper, is lightly sweet at first but has a slightly bitter aftertaste. It is used mostly in the cooking of Spain, Hungary and North Africa.

Pimentón
Pimiento is the Spanish word for pepper and *pimentón* describes the most popular seasoning, after salt, in the Spanish kitchen. It is a red powder, similar to paprika, made from dried peppers (mostly the Ñora variety) or sometimes, as in Extremadura, oak-smoked peppers. It can be either sweet—*dulce*—or pungent, which could mean hot or sour-sweet—*picante*—according to the variety of peppers from which it is made.

Antep Pepper
A common ingredient in Turkey, the brilliant red color of antep pepper seems always to add a presence to the table. It is made from a long red, slightly hot pepper which is dried and then flaked and originates from Gaziantep, in Southeast Turkey—hence its name.

Urfa Pepper
Flakes of dried pepper, like the antep, but with a darker, purple hue. This is because the pepper is lightly toasted, which also gives it a slight sourness. In Turkey urfa pepper is traditionally served with kebabs and raw onions.

PURSLANE
Purslane, with its larger silvery-colored furry leaves and thick fleshy, cacti-like stems, has a light lemony, refreshing taste and the wild variety in particular makes an unusual and refreshing salad.

It should be trimmed of the thick stems at the bottom, then both leaves and remaining stems chopped coarsely and dressed with an aromatic olive oil and lemon juice. It can also be combined with diced cucumber or with other greens. Its most notable presence is in the Lebanese bread salad Fattoush (page 138).

SWISS CHARD

Chard belongs to the same family as beetroot, sugar beet and spinach. The leaves, which have a sweet and meadowy taste, are perfect for wrapping food. As the ribbed stems of chard can be quite hard, it is best to trim them off for most purposes. They are very tasty on their own, but need longer cooking.

Like spinach, chard contains vitamin C, carotene, iron, potassium and folic acid. Swiss chard is also a very good source of fiber.

TOMATOES

It is quite a paradox that the brilliantly scarlet tomato, which is instantly associated with the Mediterranean and is indispensable to its cooking, is not a local inhabitant but an immigrant. It was brought to Spain from America by Christopher Columbus in the sixteenth century, but it did not become popular until much later. Its name is derived from the Aztec word *tomatl*, although it was originally known in Spain as *pomo d'oro*—golden apple—as the original varieties were yellow in color.

Tomatoes are low in calories, and contain a large amount of vitamin A as well as vitamins C and E, and a number of minerals such as calcium, potassium, iron and phosphorus. More importantly, they are rich in beta-carotene which is possibly the most effective antioxidant, and levels of this increase when tomatoes are grilled or roasted.

Preserved Tomatoes, Tomato Paste
and Sun-Dried Tomatoes
It was the task of my grandmother, along with the other matriarchs of our neighboring households, to preserve tomatoes in different forms at the end of each summer. First, the small plum tomatoes would be preserved whole in jars, not unlike today's familiar cans of tomatoes. However, the real task—and one that was done on a rather large scale—was making and preserving tomato paste.

Ordinary large tomatoes were cut in half and sprinkled with salt. They were then exposed to the strong summer sun for two to three days, until shriveled. They were then boiled down with more salt and finally the thick pulp was pressed through a sieve. This was stored in jars for use throughout the winter, the top of each sealed with a layer of olive oil.

For the majority of us, however, the colorful parade

of cans, jars and packets of tomatoes in the shops—whole, chopped or liquidized (when it is called passata), or the jars and tubes of tomato purée, have eliminated this task. Sun-dried tomatoes are a recent addition and originated in Italy. As described above, these tomatoes have been sliced in two, sprinkled with salt and exposed to the hot summer sun until completely dried up. Today in the south of Italy, particularly in Puglia, where quantities of sun-dried tomatoes are produced, slow ovens are often used to dry them.

Sun-dried tomatoes have a unique taste, with their concentrated sunny flavors, and they can be used to enhance a number of dishes such as pasta, salads, stuffings, etc. They can be bought dry, in which case they have to be reconstituted in warm water before use, or they come preserved in oil and ready to use.

LEGUMES

Much used in Mediterranean cooking, these are packed with protein, carbohydrates and nutrients.

BEANS

Beans are a staple in the Mediterranean, although not indigenous, since most varieties are visitors from the New World. They come in different colors, sizes and shapes. Some countries seem to favor some more than others. The most universally popular and commonly used bean is the white elongated cannellini bean. Italy, however, prefers the marbled red-and-white-skinned borlotti bean. France treasures the smaller white haricot bean. They are used in soups, in purées, in casseroles with meat and sausages and in salads.

As well as the lengthy soaking required for all legumes, most types of bean need to be boiled rapidly for a few minutes and the water then discarded before further cooking to remove toxins and make them more digestible. Beans are an excellent source of protein, calcium, iron, sodium and vitamin A.

Dried Fava Beans

These can be bought whole or skinned and flaked. They are the hardest legumes to cook, particularly when whole and unskinned. In any case they definitely have to be soaked overnight. When they are used for dishes such as the Egyptian Tamia, Lebanese Falafel, or Moroccan Byesar (pages 42-43) you need to buy the skinned variety.

CHICKPEAS

A native of the Mediterranean, they were served in ancient Greece, both as a staple and as a dessert, for which purpose they were roasted. Their nutty taste makes wonderful casseroles, soups and velvety thick dips of all kinds like the Middle Eastern Hummus (page 40). They also make excellent combinations with green vegetables, such as spinach and chard. It is perhaps in Spain, where they are called garbanzos, that they have been used most imaginatively. Chickpeas contain vitamin B, potassium and iron.

LENTILS

Natives of the Mediterranean, lentils come in different sizes and colors. They can be gray green, brown, or slate-colored and they can be large or small. I find the small green or gray-green varieties have the best flavors. French Puy lentils, one of these types, are wonderful. There are also the small Egyptian lentils, which have an orange color once skinned. Lentils have a nutty taste and they are a good source of protein, calcium, iron, selenium and vitamin A.

FRUIT

"Outside the yard is a big orchard on both sides of the gates, of four acres, and a hedge runs along each side of it, and there tall leafy trees have grown, pears and pomegranates and shiny fruited apples and sweet figs and leafy olives; and their fruit never fails winter or summer…pear upon pear grows old and apple upon apple, grapes upon grapes and fig upon fig." (Homer's *Odyssey* 7, 112-21.)

Fruit makes an astounding source of fiber and nutrients, and occasionally even more so in its dried form, like figs, apricots and raisins or currants. Fresh fruit is also very low in calories.

FIGS

Fig trees probably originated in Asia Minor, but they grow wild all over the Mediterranean as they are quite hardy with strong roots. They can survive the dry and hot summer months without need of watering and still produce their sugary fruit.

In ancient Greece the fig tree and its fruit had erotic connotations and played a strong part in folklore. With its strong smell, the tree is apparently a powerful hallucinatory source, and in Greek folklore people are not supposed to sleep under it as they may go mad. Figs were served in ancient Greece as an appetizer. Athenaeos quotes the poet Lynceus of Samos who mentions the local custom of eating figs with the appetizers rather than among the desserts. He was my inspiration for the dish of figs with mozzarella cheese on page 46. Figs contain calcium, potassium and iron.

GRAPES

Grapes have grown wild around the eastern Mediterranean and the fruit—as well as the wine made from it—has been enjoyed since antiquity. Red grapes have a high content of an antioxidant called quercetin and their skins contain a natural pesticide which when taken into the system prevents thrombosis and boosts generation of the cholesterol-lowering high-density lipoproteins (HDLs). Dried grapes—raisins—are particularly rich sources of potassium and iron.

LEMONS

The lemon probably originated in Southeast Asia, like all citrus fruits, and Tom Stobart says in his *Herbs, Spices and Flavorings* that it reached Greece and Italy by the end of the third century BC. Lemon juice is an important souring agent, but it is the lemon's zest that has the wonderful aromatic oil. The zest should be finely grated or peeled and chopped finely before use. Lemons are rich in vitamin C and they also contain a good amount of folic acid.

Most lemons on sale today have been coated in a wax containing fungicidal chemicals that prolong the life of the fruit. This is obviously advantageous for the fruit trade, but not necessarily for the human body. So, when planning to use lemon zest in a dish, it makes sense to look for unwaxed fruit.

Preserved Lemons

Pickled lemons are indispensable in Moroccan cooking, particularly for their *tajines*. They are also refreshing chopped finely into salads. One sees great glass jars filled with them in the *soukhs*. They are easy to pickle in brine at home, using a process not very different from that used to pickle olives.

LIMES

The small, bushy and thorny lime tree, like other citrus fruit trees, originated in Southeast Asia. Its fruits are round and smaller than lemons, and of a vivid green color. What distinguishes them from lemons is their strong aroma and taste, which is quite sour compared to that of a lemon. Its fragrant zest adds quite a tropical note when sprinkled over dishes.

Dried Limes

Dried limes are mainly used in the Gulf and in Iran. The best ones are those that have been left to dry on the tree. For commercial reasons, however, limes are today mostly dried artificially, which results in an inferior flavor. Even so, they add a wonderful sour taste to vegetables and meat stews.

POMEGRANATES

The pomegranate certainly wins the beauty contest among fruits. I cannot think of anything more stunning than the sparkling vermilion of the curvy pomegranate with its frilly crown. The pomegranate came from Persia, where it was first cultivated four thousand years ago.

Patience is required to extract the seeds from the skin and the bitter yellow pith. It is best to extract them to a plate and then eat them with a spoon. They are wonderful sprinkled into salads, fruit salads and all kinds of cooked dishes. Pomegranates contain a respectable amount of vitamin C.

Pomegranate Syrup

The juice of pomegranates has been used as a souring agent for centuries. It can either be used fresh or it is boiled to a paste—not to be confused with sweet syrupy Grenadine (also made from pomegranates)—for use throughout the year. It is very popular throughout the Middle East, particularly in Lebanon and Turkey where it is used for salad dressings and in dips or in vegetable casseroles. Its sweet-and-sour taste adds a new dimension to any dish.

GRAINS

BULGAR

Bulgar (also bulghur or burghul), or "cracked wheat" originated in Mesopotamia. References to it can be found in the Bible but also in some ninth-century BC Assyrian tablets, where one of the dishes mentioned is *kubba* (in Iraq) or *kibbe* (in Syria), made with cracked wheat and stuffed with meat and spices. It was also used by the ancient Greeks as *khondros*. It was the most common grain in the Middle East before the advent of imported and expensive rice.

Traditionally in the Middle East, bulgar is made by dropping wheat grains into boiling water and cooking them until almost soft. They are then drained and spread on terraces and left for three days, being stirred twice daily. The grain dries and becomes wrinkled in the heat. It is then shelled and spread in the sun again, which separates the dried husks and gives the grain a nutty taste. It is then ground coarsely. This explains why it requires little cooking.

Bulgar has been widely used in the Middle East in pilafs, in stuffings for vegetables or vine leaves, in soups, mixed with meat and made into kebabs, and in salads such as the Lebanese Tabbouleh (see page 145).

Couscous

Couscous is a tiny, round, soft, pale-yellow grain made from durum wheat flour and constitutes the Moroccan, Tunisian and Algerian national dish. In all of these countries, couscous is served with combinations of meat, poultry or fish with spices, herbs, vegetables, and perhaps dried fruit and nuts.

Most of the couscous sold today has been pre-cooked, so all one has to do is to reconstitute the grain in an amount of water (or stock) equal to its volume for fifteen to twenty minutes. Once the liquid has been absorbed, run your fingers through the grain, lifting it in the air and letting the grains tumble down to separate them and break up any lumps that have formed.

Apart from its use as the traditional accompaniment to meat, poultry or fish tajines in North Africa, couscous makes the basis for wonderful salads combined with fruit, fresh herbs and other ingredients, as in the Couscous and Peach Salad on page 83, or it can be used for stuffings.

Polenta

Polenta is the speciality of Northern Italy and particularly Venice, Lombardy and Piedmont. It never conquered the South, where pasta has remained the reigning monarch. Modern polenta—*puls* in Latin—is a mixture of corn meal and water. According to Anna Del Conte in her fascinating *Secrets from an Italian Kitchen*, polenta was originally made from a variety of cereals, and during the Renaissance, barley, chestnuts, fava beans and millet flour were used.

Corn, along with tomatoes, beans and peppers, came to Europe from the New World with Columbus. The yellow grain arrived from Spain in the Rialto market in Venice, where it was immediately christened *granoturco*—Turkish grain—for no sensible explanation other than its exotic color and its distinct foreignness. By the sixteenth century, with the decline and fall of the Eastern Empire, Venetians and the peasants of the mainland were quite poor, so this easy-to-grow crop became a staple around the Po Valley, where it was first cultivated. And so yellow polenta had arrived in Venice.

As a staple for the poor, polenta was mostly eaten by itself or sometimes with milk or butter. Leftovers were broiled and eaten for breakfast the next day, or kept for lunch, when they might be adorned with cheap accompaniments, such as beans, onions, lard or crackling, and, for those who could afford it, *baccalà*—salt cod. This was *cucina povera* in all its inventiveness.

Polenta, with its soft texture and mild taste, makes an ideal background for juxtaposing bold flavors. Its versatility lies in its constantly changing character: with melted cheese such as fontina or gorgonzola added in at the final moments of its cooking, it becomes rich and sumptuous; with a rich stew, such as the Venetian classic *polenta con seppie nere* (polenta with cuttlefish in its own ink or squid, as on page 78), it becomes dynamic.

HERBS & SPICES

BASIL *Ocimum basilicum*

In his book *Herbs, Spices and Flavorings*, Tom Stobart suggests that basil may have come to Europe from India via the Middle East. It has holy associations, and in Greece small bunches of the herb are used in church to sprinkle holy water and often to adorn icons.

Basil is probably the most important herb in the kitchen and it is the Italians who have used it most. In Genoese Pesto (page 33)—the basil-based sauce for pasta—it comes into its own. It also has a wonderful affinity with tomatoes. Its sweet aroma is unparalleled and it can transform a simple tomato sauce into an exotic delicacy. It is best to tear basil by hand rather than chopping it with a knife, as this bruises it.

CORIANDER/CILANTRO *Coriandrum sativum*

Coriander is indigenous to the Mediterranean area. It was used medicinally by Hippocrates in ancient Greece, and seeds of it were found in the Franhthi cave in Argolis which dates them at about 7000 BC. Both its fresh leaves (cilantro) and its small round brown-colored seeds (coriander), with their warm aroma, are used in cooking, particularly in the Middle East and North Africa. The seeds are used whole or ground in savory and sweet dishes and for pickling.

CUMIN *Cuminum cyminum*

In the Mediterranean, cumin is among the most popular of spices. Its presence is made unmistakable by its powerful aroma. I regard cumin as a cool spice with an elegant taste. It originated in Egypt and the

Middle East and then spread eastward and westward. Its light colored green-gray seeds can be used either whole or ground, but they always taste richer when they have been roasted first.

MARJORAM AND OREGANO *Origanum majorana; O. vulgare*
Native to the Mediterranean, these small woody plants, with their tiny leaves and small white flowers, grow wild on hillsides and in disused fields. Known in Greece as *rigani*, oregano is loved by all and is indispensable in the kitchen. It is a favorite in everything from roasts and kebabs to pizzas, casseroles and marinades. This is the herb that I could not cook without. Even in the depths of winter its aroma can instantly transport me to a Greek hillside.

PARSLEY *Petroselinum sativum*
Parsley originated in the eastern Mediterranean and it was used in ancient Greece and Rome. It is the most popular herb around the Mediterranean and is added to almost every dish. It is a good source of beta-carotene. The flat-leaved variety is the type used in the Mediterranean and it is considered to have much better flavor than the curly-leaved variety.

SAFFRON *Crocus sativus*
The golden-orange colored threads of saffron are the dried stigmas of the autumnal purple-colored flowers of the crocus plants. They make the most expensive aromatic ingredient in the world because both flowers and stigmas are hand-picked and it takes about 6,000 of them to produce 1 ounce of saffron. Jill Norman in her book *Spices* says that it was probably first cultivated in Asia Minor as it was used by the ancient Egyptians, Greeks and Romans.

The best saffron now comes from Spain, where it was introduced by the Arabs around the tenth century. Saffron has an unmistakable aroma and a slightly bitter taste. A pinch of threads will color a whole dish bright golden. It is preferable to buy threads to safeguard against adulteration.

OTHER FLAVORING INGREDIENTS
ANCHOVIES
Slim, elongated, silvery-blue anchovies, either fresh or salted, are prized throughout the Mediterranean. It is a cheap fish, but a gastronome's dream. The beloved *boquerones* of Spanish cuisine, the *hamsi* of Turkish and the *gavros* of Greek are baked with garlic, olive oil, lemon and oregano, or they are fried crisp.

Anchovies are ubiquitous around the Mediterranean in their salted form. Today, however, they are more familiar as fillets preserved in brine in jars or in tins with olive oil. There is no doubt that the best are the dried salted ones, which should be rinsed properly before use. People who object to the strong taste of anchovies occasionally marinate them in milk before rinsing.

Salted anchovies will liven up the most frugal of meals, which explains their popularity since ancient times. They are used in pizzas, with pasta, in salads such as Salade Niçoise (page 136). Pounded, they make the French *anchoïade* and the Piedmontese *bagna caôda*.

CAPERS
Capers grow wild all around the Mediterranean where they have been used for thousands of years. The small pretty bush often appears to be trailing as it prefers to grow from high ground. It has large pink flowers that resemble those of the lily or wild rose, and they are ephemeral—flowering in the morning and gone by the evening. On the Aegean island of Santorini, where they are proud of their capers, they also pickle the young caper shoots and serve them with olive oil as a

special *mezze* called *kaparofylla*. Capers can be either pickled in brine or dry-salted.

HARISSA

This North African condiment, traditionally served with couscous, is basically a chili and garlic sauce and can easily be made by puréeing chilies with garlic and some ground coriander seeds and cumin.

MASTIC

Mastic is the solid gum or resin from the bark of the evergreen tree *Pistacia lentiscus*, which grows mainly on the Greek island of Chios but also in some parts of the Middle East. The word comes from the Greek word *masso*—to chew, hence to masticate.

Its flavor and aroma—like freshly ironed linen I think—is essential to a number of Greek breads and cakes. It is wonderful in ice cream and used to be the traditional flavoring in Turkish Delight.

RAS EL HANOUT

This is a formidable mixture of about twenty-five spices, herbs and dried flowers. Many of them—such as ash berries, monk's pepper and cantharides—possessing medicinal or aphrodisiacal qualities. It also contains cinnamon, cardamom, cloves, turmeric, ginger, lavender flowers and cumin. Today it is mostly bought ready-made in the markets. It is used in kebabs, couscous and rice dishes, and in tajines for its warming effect.

ROSE WATER

Roses probably originated in ancient Persia and Babylon. Persia apparently was exporting rose water and rose wine to distant places, such as China, two thousand years ago. It was the Persians and the Arabs who developed a taste for rose water, which they used not only for medicinal purposes, in perfumes and cosmetics, but in all kinds of dishes from pilafs to desserts. Rose water came to Europe with the Crusaders. It is extracted from the petals either by steam distillation under pressure or water. According to food writer Helen Saberi, it takes thirty roses to produce one drop of oil or 60,000 roses for one ounce.

SUMAC

This is the sour red berry of a wild bush (*Rhus coriaria*) which grows all over the Middle East. It is dried to a deep burgundy color for use either whole or ground. Sumac has a pleasantly mild but definite fruity sour taste and is sprinkled over fish, kebabs, or salads such as Fattoush (page 138) to add another layer of flavor. Chopped raw onions are often rolled in sumac berries as an accompaniment to kebabs.

TAHINI

Tahini is made from roasted, pulped sesame seeds. It is used extensively in the Middle East in dishes such as Hummus (page 40) and *mezze* such as Tahinosalata (page 46). It is extremely nutritious.

VINEGAR

Vinegar is any alcoholic liquid which has become sour by the action of acid-forming bacteria. The word is derived from the French *vin aigre*, or sour wine. Vinegar made from fermented grape juice has been used in the Mediterranean since ancient times. Today, the two aristocrats of vinegar are the Italian balsamic and the Spanish sherry vinegar.

Balsamic is made mainly in Modena, from Trebbiano grapes which possess an ebony color, a syrupy consistency and full spicy bouquet. The process starts with fresh grape must, which is boiled down in order to concentrate the sugar content and flavor. A respectable balsamic vinegar should be aged in wood for at least six years (some say twelve) for its flavors to develop.

Spanish sherry vinegar, made in Jerez from the Palomino grapes, is dark and smooth with a rounded caramel taste, but it is not as sweet as balsamic.

NUTS

PINE NUTS

Pine nuts are the seeds contained inside the cones of a certain pine tree, the *Pinus pinea*, which is indigenous to the Mediterranean. Once the seeds have come out of the cone they have a woody skin like a pistachio nut, which has to be cracked in order to remove the nut. So, collecting pine nuts is very labor-intensive, which explains their high price. Their delicately sweet creamy, smooth taste combines so well with all kinds of ingredients—from vegetables to fruit and pasta— that they are one of the most important items in the pantry. They should, however, be bought in small quantities and stored in a cool, dark, dry spot, as they don't keep well and readily go rancid.

I prefer to toast pine nuts lightly before use, as this gives them a nuttier flavor and a crisper texture. They are used in a number of sweet and savory dishes in the Middle East, Turkey and North Africa. In Lebanon, one finds them in almost every dish. Sprinkled over salads or fruit salads, toasted pine nuts add quite an exotic note. Although rich in calories, a few pine nuts go a long way.

PISTACHIO NUTS

These are the fruit of a rather small tree, *Pistacia vera*, and they appear in clusters in the spring. The inner kernel of a pistachio has a beautiful green color and a very delicate nutty taste. The love for pistachios is proverbial in the Arab countries, where they are used as filling for a number of honey-drenched desserts like *baklava*. They are a labor-intensive and fragile crop, and their price is correspondingly high. However, even a small quantity used in a dish will add an exquisite note. They are used in both sweet and savory dishes: they are sprinkled over *pilafs* in Middle Eastern countries and in Turkey; they are delicious sprinkled over ice cream and fruit salads; and they are also used in Turkish Delight or in mouth-watering caramelized clusters. The stout fleshy Persian pistachio nuts are among the best.

DAIRY PRODUCTS

FETA CHEESE

Greek feta cheese is a soft but firm brilliantly white cheese made, ideally, from sheep or goat milk. It has a sharp, lightly salty taste and a fragrance that I love. A good feta is extremely appetizing. In Greece it is ubiquitous, as it is served at all times of the day—for breakfast, for *mezze*, for lunch, at dinner, and in between for snacks as well. It is also crumbled and used in stuffings for pies, from cheese pies to zucchini or spinach pies and over salads.

HALOUMI

Traditionally, Cypriot haloumi was made either from goat's or sheep's milk. Today, haloumi is exported from Cyprus in two forms, the fresh variety and the hard or aged variety. It is mostly made with a combination of primarily cows' milk and some sheep's milk. The fresh variety, which has a shorter shelf-life and is sold pre-packed, has an unmistakable elastic texture and a savory salty taste. It is eaten fresh—it goes well with tomatoes—but it is at its best sliced and grilled, either over charcoal or on a ridged heavy cast-iron pan. It can be fried in olive oil and served as part of a *mezze*, or it may be fried with eggs. If it is too salty for your taste, rinse it under cold water before using.

The older, matured variety is normally kept in brine in tins and sold by weight. This cheese is fairly hard in texture and quite salty. It is mainly used grated over pasta dishes, with a little mint, and for a Cypriot version of ravioli as well as for grilling.

Mozzarella Cheese

Mozzarella is ideally made from buffalo milk and has a rich sweet taste and a pleasing soft texture. Because of its melting qualities, it makes for very good toppings for baked dishes and is excellent combined with tomatoes—both characteristics combining memorably in that Italian classic, the pizza.

Parmesan Cheese

Parmesan is the best-known among Italian cheeses and one of the most tasty cheeses in the world. It is made mostly in Parma but also in Bologna and Modena. It is matured for between eighteen months and two years before going into the market and its production is governed by strict regulations. It should have a mellow rich flavor and a satisfying crumbly texture. The large wheels exported from Italy will always have the words "Parmigiano-reggiano" printed on the side. When grated Parmesan is called for in a dish, it is infinitely better to grate it fresh.

Pecorino

Pecorino is an Italian cheese that comes from ewes' milk—hence its name, *pecora* meaning sheep—and is produced in different regions of Italy. It has different flavors, from soft, sweet and mellow to harder, more savory and salty. The cheese made in Tuscany is called Pecorino Toscano and that from Sardinia, Pecorino Sardo. Pecorino Romano, made in and around Rome, can be quite hard and a bit too salty.

The textures and tastes of the cheeses vary, firstly because of the feed on which the ewes will have been grazing, but more importantly because of its degree of maturity. The fresh variety can be between one and two months old and the harder and more pungent, saltier variety will be about six months old.

It is important to taste the cheese before buying it. For instance, when using it to make pesto, a fresher, milder variety would be best. For pasta fillings, such as the Chard Cannelloni with Pine Nuts on page 64, the harder, more mature variety is preferred.

Ricotta

Ricotta is a fresh white cheese made from whey. It should be soft, creamy and sweet-tasting. Because of its fresh character, it should be used quickly as it is extremely perishable and acquires a sour taste and a yellow color when old. It is extremely useful in stuffings, sweets or served with fruit.

Yogurt

Yogurt is made by causing milk to ferment by the introduction of the active bacteria *lactobacillus bulgaricus* and *streptococcus thermophilus*. It was brought to the West by the Nomadic Turks; there are mentions of yogurt in seventh-century texts.

Yogurt is nourishing, it helps digestion, it is soothing to the nerves and it is believed to have therapeutic qualities, particularly for intestinal trouble. All in all, it is a general restorative. It is eaten daily in Turkey and the Middle East, where it can be found in many salads and dips. It is also popular in Greece, where a bowl of creamy yogurt is often served with thick honey and topped with walnuts. In Turkey, it is made into a cooling drink called *ayran*.

Yogurt is rich in vitamins B_2 and B_{12}, also vitamin A if it is full-fat. It is also full of protein and calcium.

Breads & Basics

SAVORY OLIVE BREAD

This is a very unusual recipe that comes from my Greek-Cypriot friend Vera Kyriakou and which I haven't encountered anywhere else in this form. Freshly baked, these crusty rolls are magnificent; cold, they are unforgettably robust! They are excellent for a picnic but also good with drinks before dinner.

Once baked, they can be frozen, then allowed to thaw for a couple of hours before being warmed up in the oven. One word of warning: do not use sharp olives soaked in vinegar—such as the Greek Kalamata—but an oily or wrinkly type. The olives can be used with the pits, but do warn people.

MAKES *about 22 rolls*

PREPARATION *about 30 minutes, plus 45 minutes' proofing*

COOKING *about 30 minutes*

Calories per serving *232*
Total fat *Medium*
Saturated fat *Low*
Protein *Low*
Carbohydrate *Medium*
Cholesterol *None*
Vitamins *Folate, A, E,*
Minerals *Calcium,*
Selenium, Potassium

3 CUPS OILY OLIVES, PREFERABLY PITTED

1 POUND FRESH SPINACH, TRIMMED

½ POUND ONIONS, PEELED, OR

7-8 SCALLIONS, TRIMMED

LARGE HANDFUL OF FRESH CILANTRO, TRIMMED

1 OUNCE FRESH YEAST

2½ CUPS WARM WATER

8 CUPS ALL-PURPOSE OR WHOLE-WHEAT FLOUR

⅔ CUP OLIVE OIL

½ TEASPOON SALT

ABOUT 2 TABLESPOONS VEGETABLE OIL

1 If the olives have been kept in brine they will be extremely salty and will first have to be rinsed briefly. Chop the spinach, onions or scallions, and cilantro finely.

2 In a bowl, dissolve the yeast in half the warm water. Let it stand for 10 minutes. In another large bowl, mix the flour, olive oil and half the salt and rub together. Add the yeast solution, mix well, and knead with your knuckles for 10 minutes. Keep adding more of the warm water as necessary. You may not need all of it, but the dough should be quite wet and sticky.

3 In a separate bowl, mix all the chopped greenery with the drained olives and remaining salt. Add to the dough, mix well, and knead again until all is well incorporated.

4 Cover the dough with a clean cloth and then a blanket, and let it rest in a warm place for about 45 minutes, or until it is well risen.

5 Preheat the oven to 425°F. Oil a baking tray with a little vegetable oil, and also oil your hands to prevent the dough from sticking to them. Form the dough into large rolls, about 3 inches across. Arrange on the baking sheet. (You can usually only fit about twelve at a time on a sheet, so—as they have to be baked in the middle of a conventional oven—you may have to bake in two batches; if you have a fan-assisted oven you can bake two sheets at a time.) Keep oiling your hands while you are working.

6 Place the baking sheet(s) in the oven and bake for 15 minutes. Then turn the heat down to 375°F and bake for another 15 minutes, until the rolls are nicely brown.

Clockwise from the left: Savory Olive Bread, Tuscan Bread with Rosemary and Olive Oil (page 30), Pizza Napoletana (page 31)

TUSCAN BREAD WITH ROSEMARY AND OLIVE OIL

This is the recipe of my friend Cecile Harris, who is an inspirational cook and baker. She often made this bread for us when we stayed with her in Tuscany. There she had the luxury of an outdoor wood-burning oven, which produced mouthwatering results. This is a very tasty bread, easy to make, and delicious toasted. So it is a good candidate for bruschetta and crostini. One often encounters rosemary in breads from Tuscany, but Cecile makes it with all kinds of additions, such as sun-dried tomatoes or walnuts. You could also use half whole-wheat flour and half white. Italian flour, which contains much more gluten, achieves the best results; it can be found in specialist stores. (See page 29.)

MAKES *2 round loaves or 1 large one*

PREPARATION *about 30 minutes, plus 1¼- 1½ hours' resting and proofing*

COOKING *45-60 minutes*

Calories per serving *193*
Total fat *Low*
Saturated fat *Low*
Protein *Low*
Carbohydrate *High*
Cholesterol *None*
Vitamins *Folate, B1*
Minerals *Iron, Selenium*

2½ CUPS WARM WATER
1 OUNCE FRESH YEAST
5 CUPS BREAD FLOUR, PLUS A LITTLE EXTRA FOR KNEADING AND DUSTING
½ CUP OLIVE OIL (PLUS MORE IF USING MOLD)

2 TABLESPOONS SALT
3-4 TABLESPOONS FRESH ROSEMARY NEEDLES, CHOPPED, OR 2 TABLESPOONS DRIED ROSEMARY
KOSHER SALT, FOR SPRINKLING

1 Place the water in a large bowl and dissolve the yeast in it. Leave for 10 minutes until frothy.
2 Add the flour, followed by the oil, salt and rosemary. Stir until it is all mixed together. Place the dough on a floured surface and knead by hand for 10 minutes, adding a little more flour as needed until it forms a smooth and elastic dough. Cover the dough and let it rest for 45 minutes in a warm place.
3 Punch the dough down a few times, flattening it, then divide it in two; either put each half in a lightly oiled rectangular 5 cup loaf pan or form each into a loaf shape. Place the loaves on a floured baking sheet and cover with a clean cloth. (A word of advice: if the weather is hot the dough will tend to be loose

and spread all over the place, so it has to be contained. In this case the loaf pan is the best solution, or you can put a ring around each loaf to contain it.) Let the dough rise for 30-40 minutes in a warm place.
4 Preheat the oven to 450°F. Steam is essential for a crusty loaf, so put a dish of boiling water on the lower shelf of the oven. Sprinkle the kosher salt on top of the dough just before baking and bake for 45-60 minutes. To see if a loaf is done, take it out of any mold being used and tap it at the base; it should sound hollow. If it isn't ready, place it back on the baking sheet upside down—without any pan—and bake a little longer. Let the loaf cool on a wire rack.

PIZZA

Traditionally pizza is baked on a brick or stone surface in a wood-fired oven, so the dough crisps from the intense heat. The best alternative is to use a baking stone, which are now more available. (See page 29.)

1 CUP BREAD FLOUR

1 CUP WHOLE-WHEAT FLOUR

1 TEASPOON SALT

1 TEASPOON ACTIVE DRY YEAST

2/3 CUP WARM WATER

1 TABLESPOON OLIVE OIL

FOR PIZZA MARGHERITA:

2 TABLESPOONS OLIVE OIL

1¼ POUNDS RIPE TOMATOES, TRIMMED AND SLICED IN THICK WEDGES, OR 14-OUNCE CAN OF TOMATOES, DRAINED

1 TEASPOON EACH DRIED OREGANO AND THYME

SALT AND FRESHLY GROUND BLACK PEPPER

5 OUNCES MOZZARELLA CHEESE, COARSELY GRATED

2 TABLESPOONS GRATED PARMESAN CHEESE

FOR PIZZA NAPOLETANA:

1¼ POUNDS RIPE TOMATOES, TRIMMED AND SLICED IN THICK WEDGES, OR 14-OUNCE CAN OF TOMATOES, DRAINED

1 TEASPOON EACH DRIED OREGANO AND THYME

SEVERAL TORN BASIL LEAVES

5-6 ANCHOVY FILLETS, CUT INTO PIECES

1 TABLESPOON OLIVE OIL

8-10 SMALL BLACK OLIVES

SERVES *4-6*

PREPARATION *about 30 minutes, plus 30 minutes' proofing*

COOKING *about 30 minutes*

Calories per serving *268*
Total fat *Medium*
Saturated fat *Medium*
Protein *Medium*
Carbohydrate *Low*
Cholesterol *11 mg*
Vitamins *A, C, E, B group*
Minerals *Iron, Zinc, Selenium, Calcium, Potassium*

1 Put the flours in a bowl and mix in salt and yeast. Add the water and oil and mix with a knife to a soft dough. Knead for 5 minutes on a floured surface. Cover and leave 5 minutes.

2 Knead the dough again on a floured surface for 3-4 minutes until soft and elastic. With the use of a rolling pin and by pulling and stretching by hand, shape the dough into either a large oblong shape or an 11-inch round. It should be very thin, about ¼ inch, and with a slightly raised rim. Place the dough on an oiled baking sheet, cover, and leave to rise for 30 minutes in the kitchen.

3 Preheat the oven to 450°F at least 20 minutes ahead of cooking. If you have a baking stone, place it in the upper shelf of the oven and preheat it too. Add any favorite topping just before the pizza is to be baked, otherwise it will become soggy.

4 To make Pizza Margherita: heat the oil in a frying pan, add the tomatoes, and turn with a spatula for 2-3 minutes over moderate heat. Add herbs, salt, and pepper, and cook for 5-6 minutes more, stirring occasionally, until fresh tomatoes look wilted and most of the liquid has evaporated. Lift tomatoes out with a slotted spoon, leaving excess juices behind, and spread evenly over the pizza. Sprinkle mozzarella on top, followed by Parmesan.

5 To make Pizza Napoletana: prepare the tomatoes as above and spread them evenly on the dough. Sprinkle with basil and add the anchovies. Sprinkle with olive oil and scatter the black olives over the top.

6 Bake either pizza for 15 minutes on the upper shelf of the oven, placing it directly on the stone if you are using one, until the dough appears crisp and golden.

SALSA DI POMODORO
Italian Tomato Sauce

This is the queen of the standby sauces as it can be made quickly and is very versatile. Its main role is with pasta of any kind, or with polenta. The list of potential uses however, is much more varied than this. It can be spread over potatoes or other vegetables and baked in the oven like a gratin. It can be spread over steaks of fish, such as cod, or over whole mackerel and baked in the oven as is done in Greece and Turkey. Alternatively, you can beat 3-4 eggs and combine them with some of this sauce, then cook the mixture like scrambled eggs for a version of the Greek strapatsatha, *from the island of Corfu. For a North African flavor, spread some of this sauce in a frying pan, break 4 whole eggs on top, sprinkle some paprika and ground cumin on each egg, cover, and cook slowly until set.*

When I make this as a pasta sauce for 4 people, I use two cans of tomatoes so that the pasta is lusciously coated. I find one can is a little scant. Whatever is not used can be stored in a refrigerator for about 4 days, or frozen. I also purée the tomatoes first, as I find the velvety consistency of the sauce much more appealing, but you don't have to do that if in a hurry—simply use cans of ready-chopped tomatoes. Of course the sauce can be made with fresh tomatoes, as we do in the summer, and then it becomes totally captivating. You will need at least 2 pounds (or more) of ripe tomatoes, skinned, seeded, and chopped, and cooked a little longer.

MAKES *about 2½ cups*

PREPARATION
10 minutes

COOKING *about 40 minutes*

Calories per serving *112*
Total fat *High*
Saturated fat *Low*
Protein *Low*
Carbohydrate *Low*
Cholesterol *None*
Vitamins *B6, E*
Minerals *Iron, Potassium*

2-3 TABLESPOONS OLIVE OIL

1 MEDIUM ONION, FINELY CHOPPED

2 GARLIC CLOVES, MINCED

1 TEASPOON DRIED OREGANO

2 (14-OZ) CANS OF TOMATOES (WITH THEIR LIQUID), PURÉED

½ TEASPOON SOFT BROWN (OR WHITE) SUGAR

SALT AND FRESHLY GROUND BLACK PEPPER

1 TABLESPOON TOMATO PASTE

HOT WATER

3-4 SPRIGS OF FRESH BASIL, TORN BY HAND, OR 3 TABLESPOONS CHOPPED PARSLEY

1 Heat the oil gently in a medium saucepan and sauté the onion until translucent. Add the garlic and oregano and, as soon as the garlic aroma rises, add the tomatoes, sugar, and salt and pepper to taste.

2 Cover the mixture and cook gently for 15 minutes, stirring occasionally. Add the tomato paste and cook for 15 more minutes, adding a little hot water if needed. Stir the sauce often at this stage in case it sticks. It should be quite smooth and thick by the end.

3 Remove the thickened sauce from the heat and mix in the torn fresh basil or chopped parsley.

PESTO

A book on Mediterranean food cannot be complete without a recipe for delicious pesto. It is the most wonderful sauce ever invented and we owe it to the Genoese. It is they who specify that for proper pesto the small-leaved variety of basil is the best. My grandmother, although she had never heard of—or made—pesto in her time, always maintained that the small-leaved variety, which she kept on every windowsill and in the garden, was superior.

Pesto may be used with any pasta, although it works best with large flat ribbons like fettuccine or with tubular pasta such as penne, which will hold larger quantities of the sauce. On the other hand, in the summer when basil is plentiful I tend to serve it with almost everything—with zucchini, potato salad, soup, rice pilaf, and so on. (See page 35.)

2 OUNCES BASIL LEAVES
1 LARGE GARLIC CLOVE, MINCED
1½ TABLESPOONS PINE NUTS
3 TABLESPOONS OLIVE OIL

1 OUNCE PARMESAN CHEESE, FRESHLY GRATED
1 TABLESPOON FRESHLY GRATED PECORINO SARDO OR ROMANO CHEESE

1 Place all the ingredients except the cheeses in a food processor and give it a quick burst. Stop and scrape everything down and repeat. If the sauce appears too dry, add 1 tablespoon of water.
2 When the sauce has a creamy appearance, add both the grated cheeses and give it one more rapid burst.
3 Keep the sauce refrigerated until needed. Just before using it, dilute it a little by adding either 2 tablespoons of the hot pasta cooking water or just plain warm water.

MAKES *6½ ounces*

PREPARATION *5-10 minutes*

Calories per tablespoon *45*
Total fat *High*
Saturated fat *High*
Protein *Low*
Carbohydrate *Low*
Cholesterol *3 mg*
Vitamins *A, E*
Minerals *Calcium, Iron, Zinc, Potassium*

SARIMSAKLI YOGURT
Yogurt and Garlic Sauce

As it can be made easily and speedily, this sauce from Turkey is a good standby. It can be served not only with vegetables and legumes but also with meat dishes, and it always adds an appetizing aspect to the meal.

1 CUP THICK LOW-FAT NATURAL YOGURT
2 GARLIC CLOVES, CRUSHED

5-6 MINT LEAVES, FINELY CHOPPED
PINCH OF PAPRIKA, TO GARNISH (OPTIONAL)

1 Beat the yogurt and garlic together in a bowl. Mix in the mint, cover and refrigerate.
2 Serve lightly chilled, garnished with a little paprika if you wish.

MAKES *8 ounces*

PREPARATION *5 minutes, plus chilling*

Calories per tablespoon *9*
Total fat *Low*
Saturated fat *Low*
Protein *High*
Carbohydrate *Medium*
Cholesterol *1 mg*
Vitamins *Negligible*
Minerals *Iodine, Calcium*

SKORTHALIA

MAKES *about 6½ ounces*

PREPARATION *10 minutes, plus 10 minutes' soaking*

Calories per tablespoon *117*
Total fat *High*
Saturated fat *Low*
Protein *Low*
Carbohydrate *Low*
Cholesterol *None*
Vitamins *Folate, E*
Minerals *Calcium, Iron, Zinc*

In Greek island homes this garlic sauce is indispensable for livening up a frugal meal of boiled vegetables, fried fish or, particularly, salt cod or fried vegetables. Skorthalia *has been consumed in Greece since ancient times. It also appears all over the Mediterranean in various forms and under different names, such as* tarator *in Turkey and the Middle East,* agliata *in Italy and* aïoli *in France.*

3 MEDIUM SLICES OF CRUSTLESS BREAD, SOAKED IN WATER FOR 10 MINUTES
2-3 GARLIC CLOVES, MINCED
1 TABLESPOON WHITE WINE VINEGAR

SALT
2 TABLESPOONS OLIVE OIL
½ CUP GROUND WALNUTS OR ALMONDS (OPTIONAL)
PINCH OF PAPRIKA, TO GARNISH (OPTIONAL)

1 Squeeze most of the water from the bread. Place it in a blender with the garlic, vinegar, and salt to taste. Then blend until smooth.
2 With the machine still running, dribble in the oil. Add the nuts, if they are used, and blend briefly. The sauce should be runny.
3 Served garnished with a little paprika if you wish.

ROUILLE

The rouille *that accompanies Provençal fish soups, particularly* Bouillabaisse, *is a fiery orange-colored mayonnaise made with garlic and chili. It is spread on croutons which are floated on top of or mixed into the soup. A substantial amount of olive oil is usually needed for this sauce, but I have cut down the amount and instead used bread and ground nuts as thickening agents.*

MAKES *about 6½ ounces*

PREPARATION *5-10 minutes, plus soaking*

Calories per tablespoon *96*
Total fat *High*
Saturated fat *Medium*
Protein *Low*
Carbohydrate *Low*
Cholesterol *31 mg*
Vitamins *A, B12*
Minerals *Iron*

1 FRESH OR DRIED RED CHILI, SEEDED AND CHOPPED
1 MEDIUM CRUSTLESS SLICE OF BREAD, SOAKED IN WATER FOR 10 MINUTES
2 GARLIC CLOVES, CHOPPED
1 EGG YOLK

1 TABLESPOON GROUND ALMONDS
1 TEASPOON TOMATO PASTE
½ TEASPOON EACH PAPRIKA AND CAYENNE PEPPER
4 TABLESPOONS OLIVE OIL
SALT

1 If using a dried chili, first soak it in a little boiling water for 30 minutes.
2 Place the chili in a food processor (if dried add a little of its liquid). Squeeze excess water from the bread and add it in together with the remaining ingredients except for the oil. Add salt to taste. Process to a smooth paste.
3 With the machine still running, dribble in the oil slowly to form a thick and creamy sauce. If it is too thick, add a little cold water.
4 Taste the sauce—it should be fiery—and adjust the seasoning with salt and cayenne.

Clockwise from top: Skorthalia, Pesto (page 33), Rouille

AVGOLEMONO
Egg-and-Lemon Sauce

MAKES *about 1¼ cups*

PREPARATION
about 5 minutes

Calories per tablespoon *11*
Total fat *High*
Saturated fat *High*
Protein *High*
Carbohydrate *Low*
Cholesterol *25 mg*
Vitamins *B12*
Minerals *Iron, Zinc*

2 LARGE EGGS AT ROOM TEMPERATURE

JUICE OF 2 LEMONS

1 TABLESPOON CORNSTARCH MIXED IN A LITTLE WATER

1 In a bowl, beat the eggs lightly with a fork or balloon whisk. Add the lemon juice and the cornstarch, then beat together until smooth.
2 Add 2-3 small ladlefuls of liquid from the dish it is to enrich, beating together for 1 minute between each addition. By now the sauce will be warm, so you can pour it slowly back into the main dish, off the heat, stirring vigorously.
3 Warm the dish up over very, very gentle heat, otherwise the eggs may curdle, although the cornstarch will safeguard against that for a minute or so. Serve immediately.

BÉCHAMEL SAUCE

This is quite a thin béchamel as it is intended mainly for the Cannelloni on page 64, where it will thicken as it is baked for a long time. If a thicker sauce is required, add a little more flour.

MAKES *about 4½ cups*

PREPARATION *5-10 minutes*

COOKING *about 40 minutes*

Calories per serving *187*
Total fat *Medium*
Saturated fat *Medium*
Protein *Medium*
Carbohydrate *Low*
Cholesterol *71 mg*
Vitamins *A, B group*
Minerals *Calcium, Zinc, Iodine, Potassium*

3 TABLESPOONS BUTTER
½ CUP ALL-PURPOSE FLOUR
3¾ CUPS HOT SKIM MILK
SALT AND FRESHLY GROUND BLACK OR WHITE PEPPER

2 PINCHES OF FRESHLY GRATED NUTMEG
2 TABLESPOONS GRATED PARMESAN CHEESE
1 EGG, LIGHTLY BEATEN

1 In a heavy-based saucepan, melt the butter gently over very low heat. Add the flour gradually, stirring constantly with a wooden spatula. I add a couple of tablespoons of milk if the mixture looks too solid.
2 Once all the flour is in, stir for 1 more minute without letting it brown. Remove from heat and start adding the milk gradually, 2-3 tablespoons at a time, stirring constantly until it has been fully blended. This safeguards against the formation of lumps. Return to a gentle heat and continue to add the milk in this manner.
3 When all the milk has been added, season to taste. Then simmer over a low heat, stirring constantly, for another 10 minutes until the sauce has thickened enough to coat a spoon. The whole process takes about half an hour.
4 Remove the sauce from the heat and let it stand for 5 minutes. Then add the nutmeg, the Parmesan, and the egg, stirring constantly until well incorporated. Adjust the seasoning if necessary. If the sauce is going to stand a little, keep stirring it from time to time to prevent a skin forming on top, or cut a piece of plastic wrap and fit it snugly on the surface.

STOCKS

Stocks are indispensable in the making of certain dishes such as soups or risotti. They are the magic ingredient that can transform a dish, so they are worth making, particularly since stock can be prepared in advance and kept in the freezer. I do not give exact quantities, but will simply indicate what the ingredients are and how they are cooked.

VEGETABLE STOCK

For vegetable stock you will need a selection of vegetables such as onions, carrots, leeks, celery, zucchini, and a potato or two. Basically anything goes. Trim or peel each vegetable as necessary and coarsely chop them. Put them in a stock pot and add water to cover completely. Add seasoning (whole peppercorns are good for stock instead of ground pepper, as they can be strained off), bring to the boil, and simmer gently for about 40-50 minutes. Strain and discard the vegetables or use for a purée. If not using the stock immediately, it may be kept in the fridge for 3-4 days, or frozen.

CHICKEN STOCK

For a really good flavor, this must be made with a fresh chicken, particularly an older boiling fowl, or it can be made with wings and necks. If using a whole chicken, it should be cut into 4-6 pieces. Barely cover the chicken pieces with cold water, bring to the boil, and skim until clear. Add some coarsely chopped carrots, onions, and celery, some seasoning, 1-2 bay leaves, and a small bunch of fresh herbs such as oregano, thyme, or marjoram. Cook gently for 1 hour or a little longer. Strain and use the chicken for a separate meal. When cool, lift off the thin layer of fat from the surface before use.

MEAT STOCK

Ask your butcher to give you some fresh beef or veal bones, including 1 or 2 pieces of marrowbone. Rinse the bones and proceed as for chicken stock, but cook for 1½ hours.

FISH STOCK

Fishmongers will readily provide a selection of fresh trimmings (you probably need about 2 pounds) from larger fish (which should include bones, but also heads), particularly if you give them notice. Ask them not to include oily fish. Rinse everything and proceed as in the recipe for chicken stock, but cook for only 30 minutes (and no more, otherwise it may become bitter).

Mezze
& Soups

HUMMUS

This Middle Eastern chickpea dip can liven up any table with its robust and earthy taste. It could accompany a simple vegetable casserole or soup, or it could hold its place as part of a larger mezze *table.*

SERVES 6-8

PREPARATION *15 minutes, plus overnight soaking*

COOKING *about 1½ hours*

Calories per serving *133*
Total fat *High*
Saturated fat *Low*
Protein *Medium*
Carbohydrate *Low*
Cholesterol *None*
Vitamins *A, B group*
Minerals *Calcium, Zinc, Iodine, Potassium*

1½ CUPS CHICKPEAS, PICKED CLEAN AND SOAKED IN COLD WATER OVERNIGHT

2 TABLESPOONS TAHINI

2 GARLIC CLOVES, MINCED

JUICE OF 1-2 LEMONS

2 TEASPOONS GROUND CUMIN

1 TABLESPOON OLIVE OIL

SALT AND FRESHLY GROUND PEPPER

TO DRESS:

1 TEASPOON OLIVE OIL

½ TEASPOON PAPRIKA OR A LITTLE CAYENNE PEPPER

1 Rinse the chickpeas, place in a saucepan, and cover with plenty of water. Bring to a boil and skim until clear. Cover and boil the chickpeas until perfectly soft. This can take about 1½ hours (or about 20 minutes if using a pressure cooker). Drain, reserving the cooking liquid.

2 If the tahini appears separated in the jar, first mix it properly with a fork. Divide all the ingredients into two batches and place the first batch in a food processor with ⅔ cup of the chickpea cooking liquid. Process until grainy and of a runny consistency. Add a little more of the cooking liquid if necessary. Taste and adjust seasoning, then blend again briefly. Empty out on a flat platter and repeat with the remaining ingredients.

3 Drizzle a little oil over the hummus and sprinkle the paprika or cayenne on top. Serve lightly chilled or at room temperature.

YOGURT AND CUCUMBER SALAD

SERVES 4-6

PREPARATION *10 minutes, plus chilling*

Calories per serving *51*
Total fat *High*
Saturated fat *Low*
Protein *High*
Carbohydrate *Low*
Cholesterol *2 mg*
Vitamins *B₂, B₃*
Minerals *Calcium, Iodine*

This sauce is found all over the Eastern Mediterranean. Known as cacik *to the Turks or* tzatziki *to the Greeks, it can be served with vegetable- and oil-based dishes, with raw vegetables, grilled fish or meat, roasts, and salads.*

1 TABLESPOON OLIVE OIL

1 TEASPOON WINE VINEGAR

1 GARLIC CLOVE, PEELED AND CRUSHED

8 OUNCES THICK PLAIN LOW-FAT YOGURT

SALT

4-INCH PIECE OF CUCUMBER, PEELED AND GRATED

1 TABLESPOON FINELY CHOPPED FRESH MINT, PLUS MORE LEAVES TO GARNISH

1 Whisk the oil, vinegar and garlic in a bowl. Add yogurt and salt and beat until smooth.

2 Squeeze the cucumber with your hands to remove excess moisture, then mix it into the sauce with the mint. Cover and refrigerate.

3 Serve lightly chilled, garnished with mint.

Clockwise from left: Hummus, Muhammara (page 42), Yogurt and Cucumber Salad

MUHAMMARA
Turkish Walnut and Pepper Dip

This is a speciality of Gaziantep in Southeast Turkey. There they would include a red pepper paste which the matriarch of each household makes at the end of the summer and stores in jars for the winter. As it is almost impossible to buy this, I have substituted pomegranate syrup (see page 19) for that additional twist in flavor. You can make it lower in fat and calories by omitting the pistachio and pine nuts. My version is adapted from a recipe by my friend Holly Chase, an expert on all things Turkish. (See page 41.)

SERVES *6-8*

PREPARATION *about 30 minutes, plus 2-3 hours' chilling*

Calories per serving *359*
Total fat *High*
Saturated fat *Low*
Protein *Low*
Carbohydrate *Low*
Cholesterol *None*
Vitamins *A, B₁, B₃, B₆, Folate, C, E,*
Minerals *Potassium, Iron, Zinc, Selenium*

3 SLICES OF BREAD, TOASTED
1 CUP SHELLED WALNUTS, TOASTED IN A LOW OVEN FOR 10 MINUTES
3 RIPE RED PEPPERS, DESEEDED AND CHOPPED
1 GARLIC CLOVE, CRUSHED
RIND AND JUICE OF 1 LEMON
2 TABLESPOONS POMEGRANATE SYRUP (OPTIONAL)
1 TEASPOON MEDIUM-HOT PEPPER FLAKES
OR 1 SMALL GREEN CHILI, DESEEDED (OPTIONAL)
5-6 SPRIGS OF FLAT-LEAVED PARSLEY
6-7 MINT LEAVES
3 TABLESPOONS FRUITY OLIVE OIL
SALT
½ CUP UNSALTED SHELLED PISTACHIO NUTS (OPTIONAL)
½ CUP PINE NUTS, LIGHTLY TOASTED

1 Combine the bread and cooled walnuts in a food processor and reduce them to crumbs.
2 Add the chopped peppers, garlic, lemon rind and juice, pomegranate syrup and pepper flakes or chili, if using. Process together to a pulp.
3 Add the herbs (reserving a sprig of parsley for garnish) and, with the machine still running, add the oil in a steady trickle.
4 Add salt to taste and the pistachio nuts if using. Process with a quick burst so that the nuts are coarsely chopped and not powdered.
5 Chill for a couple of hours in order to let the flavors blend. Take out of the refrigerator about half an hour before serving.
6 Just before serving, mix in half of the pine nuts and turn out on a serving plate. Sprinkle the remaining pine nuts over to serve and garnish with a sprig of parsley if you wish.

BESSARA
Egyptian Purée of Fava Beans and Herbs

I was introduced to bessara *by the Egyptian chef Esmat Farid of the restaurant Valley of the Kings in West London. I was instantly captivated by its lively refreshing taste. It is one of the ancient Arab dishes to be found from Egypt to Cyprus to North Africa under slightly different names such as* byesar.

1⅓ CUPS SKINNED DRIED FAVA BEANS, PICKED CLEAN AND SOAKED OVERNIGHT IN COLD WATER
2 OUNCES EACH PARSLEY (PREFERABLY FLAT-LEAVED) AND CILANTRO, COARSELY CHOPPED
1-2 FRESH GREEN CHILIES, DESEEDED AND CHOPPED
2 GARLIC CLOVES, MINCED
1½ TEASPOONS GROUND CUMIN
3 TABLESPOONS OLIVE OIL
SALT
1 MEDIUM ONION, PEELED AND THINLY SLICED

1 Strain and rinse the beans. Place in a pan, preferably a pressure cooker, with plenty of water, and bring to the boil. Boil for 3-4 minutes and drain. Cover with fresh water by about 1 inch and cook until done. In a pressure cooker this would take 10-15 minutes, otherwise it will take about 1 hour.
2 Mix in the herbs, cover, and simmer for 5 minutes. Strain, reserving some of the liquid.
3 Combine the beans with the chilies, garlic, cumin, 2 tablespoons of oil, and 3-4 tablespoons of the reserved liquid in a food processor and process to a smooth paste. Season to taste with salt. If too dry, add a little more of the cooking liquid. Empty into a medium-sized pâté dish, cover and refrigerate.
4 Just before serving, heat the remaining oil in a non-stick pan and fry the onion briskly until golden and crisp. Spread onion over the pâté and serve with fresh bread.

SERVES 4

PREPARATION *about 15 minutes, plus overnight soaking*

COOKING *about 1¼ hours, plus cooling*

Calories per serving 230
Total fat *Medium*
Saturated fat *Low*
Protein *High*
Carbohydrate *Low*
Cholesterol *None*
Vitamins *A, B₁, B₂, B₃, B₆, Folate, C, E*
Minerals *Calcium, Iron, Zinc, Potassium*

MELITZANOSALATA

Melitzanosalata *in Greece and* baba ghanoush *in the Middle East are deliciously refreshing eggplant salads. Ideally the eggplants should be grilled on charcoal for that unmistakable smoky aroma. Here I have improvised a trick that produces at least some of the smoky flavor in the kitchen.*

2¼ POUNDS EGGPLANT
½ SMALL ONION, COARSELY CHOPPED
1-2 GARLIC CLOVES, CRUSHED
JUICE OF 1 SMALL LEMON
3 TABLESPOONS OLIVE OIL
SALT AND FRESHLY GROUND BLACK PEPPER
2 TABLESPOONS CHOPPED FLAT-LEAVED PARSLEY
4-6 BLACK OLIVES, TO GARNISH

1 Preheat the oven to 350°F. Prick the eggplants with a fork, lay them directly on the oven racks, and roast for about 1 hour, until soft and properly cooked. Turn them over twice during the process.
2 Wearing oven gloves, take the eggplant out of the oven and lay each one over a low naked flame for 2-3 minutes, turning them as they become charred. This is messy, but does impart the smoky flavor. You can omit this step altogether, or do it for a shorter time.
3 Slit the cooled eggplants open. Spoon the flesh out into a strainer and squeeze it dry.
4 Place the flesh in a food processor with the onion, garlic, and lemon juice and process rapidly. With the machine still running, dribble in the oil until a smooth paste is formed. Adjust the seasoning.
5 Spread on a serving platter, sprinkle parsley on top, and pile olives in the middle.

SERVES 4

PREPARATION *about 10 minutes*

COOKING *about 1¼ hours, plus cooling*

Calories per serving 127
Total fat *High*
Saturated fat *Medium*
Protein *Low*
Carbohydrate *Low*
Cholesterol *None*
Vitamins *B₃, Folate, C, E*
Minerals *Iron, Potassium*

ROAST ZUCCHINI WITH SALSA VERDE

Roasting zucchini transforms their flavor, as it concentrates it and they become much sweeter as a result. I make the green sauce with which they are served with a number of different fresh herbs, and of course this gives scope for individual improvisation. This dish is extremely enticing when served with Italian bread, such as ciabatta or focaccia, or even a sourdough or French baguette.

Inspired by Anna Del Conte's wonderful book Entertaining all'Italiana, *I have also treated eggplants in a very similar way to make* melanzane con salsa verde. *Top and tail the eggplants, cut into rounds about ¼-inch thick, and place these slices side by side in one layer on the baking sheet. Season the olive oil and brush the eggplants sparingly with it. Cook in the oven as below for 35-40 minutes, until the eggplant slices are soft and starting to turn golden on top. Arrange them decoratively on a pretty serving platter and, about half an hour before serving, cover the top of each eggplant slice with a thin layer of the salsa verde. This makes an appetizing dish that is ideal for a buffet table or for serving cold at an* al fresco *lunch. To make a complete meal, it can be served with the Couscous Salad with Peaches, Arugula and Pine Nuts on page 83.*

SERVES *4-6*

PREPARATION *15-20 minutes*

COOKING *50 minutes, plus cooling*

Calories per serving *72*
Total fat *High*
Saturated fat *Medium*
Protein *Low*
Carbohydrate *Low*
Cholesterol *None*
Vitamins *A, C, Folate*
Minerals *Iron, Potassium*

1½ POUNDS MEDIUM-SIZED FIRM ZUCCHINI, TRIMMED BUT KEPT WHOLE

1 TABLESPOON OLIVE OIL

FOR THE SALSA VERDE:
2 GARLIC CLOVES, MINCED

1 TABLESPOON DIJON MUSTARD

LARGE HANDFUL OF FLAT-LEAVED PARSLEY

SMALL HANDFUL OF FRESH MINT

JUICE OF ½ LEMON

2-3 TABLESPOONS OLIVE OIL

SALT

1 Preheat the oven to 375°F. Cover a baking sheet with foil, oil it lightly, and arrange the zucchini on it. Brush their tops with a little oil and roast for 50 minutes.

2 Take the zucchini out of the oven and, when they are cooled, slice them across into 2½-inch long pieces. Then, unless they are very slim, quarter each piece lengthwise to produce thin batons. Place the pieces in a large bowl.

3 While the zucchini is cooling, make the salsa: place all the ingredients, apart from the olive oil and a sprig or two of mint, in a food processor with salt to taste and work into a smooth paste. With the machine still running, slowly add in the olive oil and blend until well emulsified to a thick pesto-like sauce.

4 Shortly before the salad is to be served, add the sauce to the zucchini and toss gently to coat. Garnish with the remaining mint.

Roast Zucchini with Salsa Verde

MARINATED MOZZARELLA WITH BARBA NIKOS'S FIG SLICES

This is an exotic personal improvisation that we serve at our Greek island home in the summer. Of course, we lack the mozzarella there so we have to substitute feta. We have this dish as a first course in the middle of August, when the figs on our trees are at their fullest. Even better when our elderly friend, one-toothed Barba Nikos, arrives with presents from his majestic hundred-year-old fig tree.

SERVES 4

PREPARATION 10 minutes, plus 2-4 hours' marinating

Calories per serving 220
Total fat *High*
Saturated fat *High*
Protein *Medium*
Carbohydrate *Low*
Cholesterol *24 mg*
Vitamins *A, B2, B12, E*
Minerals *Calcium, Zinc, Potassium*

5 OUNCES BUFFALO MOZZARELLA CHEESE

5-6 FIRM FIGS

6-8 MINT LEAVES

SALT AND FRESHLY GROUND BLACK PEPPER

FOR THE MARINADE:

2 TABLESPOONS WALNUT OIL

1 TEASPOON SUNFLOWER OIL

JUICE OF 1 LEMON

½ GARLIC CLOVE, PEELED AND CRUSHED

1 Slice the cheese thinly. Beat the marinade ingredients lightly together in a bowl and season to taste. Coat the cheese slices in marinade, cover, and chill for 2-4 hours.
2 Just before serving, take the cheese out of the refrigerator. Trim both ends of each fig

and slice each one in about 3-4 round slices. Arrange the cheese and fig slices decoratively on a round platter.
3 Dribble the marinade all over and scatter the mint on top.

TAHINOSALATA

Tahini is made from crushed sesame seeds and brings an exotic taste to anything to which it is added. Tahinosalata is a sharp and appetizing dip to be offered with vegetable crudités or hot pita bread.

SERVES 4-6

PREPARATION 10 minutes

Calories per serving 90
Total fat *High*
Saturated fat *Medium*
Protein *Low*
Carbohydrate *Low*
Cholesterol *None*
Vitamins *B1, B3, Folate*
Minerals *Iron, Calcium*

4 TABLESPOONS TAHINI

⅔ CUP WARM WATER

2 GARLIC CLOVES, MINCED

½ TEASPOON GROUND CUMIN

1-2 TABLESPOONS OLIVE OIL

JUICE OF 1 LEMON

SALT

BLACK OLIVES, TO GARNISH

1 If the tahini in the jar looks separated, stir to mix it. Measure the tahini, water, garlic, and cumin into a food processor or blender. Season and process briefly.
2 With the machine still running, start slowly

adding the olive oil and lemon juice alternately, until the mixture looks creamy.
3 Adjust the seasoning and empty into a bowl. Garnish with the olives and serve. It will keep, covered, in the refrigerator for 3-4 days.

Marinated Mozzarella with Barba Nikos's Fig Slices

TYROPITAKIA LEFTERITSAS

These little cheese pies used to be made for us by an Athenian friend called Eleftheria, meaning "liberty," hence their name. Cold, the pies are ideal for picnics.

FOR THE PASTRY:

1¾ CUPS SELF-RISING FLOUR, SIFTED

2 TABLESPOONS OLIVE OIL

1 TABLESPOON MELTED BUTTER

3 OUNCES PLAIN THICK LOW-FAT YOGURT

1 TEASPOON VEGETABLE OIL , TO GREASE THE PAN

1 EGG YOLK, LIGHTLY BEATEN, TO GLAZE

FOR THE FILLING:

5 OUNCES FETA CHEESE, CRUMBLED WITH A FORK

1 LARGE EGG, LIGHTLY BEATEN

2 TABLESPOONS FINELY CHOPPED DILL OR MINT

1 SCALLION, FINELY CHOPPED

FRESHLY GROUND BLACK PEPPER

MAKES *12-15*

PREPARATION *about 35 minutes, plus 15 minutes' resting*

COOKING *20 minutes,*

Calories per pie *108*
Total fat *High*
Saturated fat *High*
Protein *Low*
Carbohydrate *Low*
Cholesterol *39 mg*
Vitamins *B group*
Minerals *Calcium, Iron, Iodine*

1 Put the flour, oil, butter, and yogurt for the pastry in a bowl and mix by hand. Add a little more flour if the mixture is too wet. Cover and let rest in the refrigerator for 15 minutes.
2 Preheat the oven to 375°F and grease a baking sheet with the vegetable oil. In another bowl, combine the filling ingredients.
3 On a lightly-floured surface, roll out one-third of the pastry, not too thinly. Using a glass or pastry cutter, cut out 3-inch circles.
4 Place a teaspoon of filling along the middle of each pastry disc, then fold it over to make a small half-moon shape. Press the edges together to seal them. Place the pies on the baking sheet. Continue with the remaining pastry and filling until they are all used up.
5 Brush the tops with egg yolk and bake for 20 minutes, until golden. Serve hot or cold.

TAPENADE
Provençal Olive and Caper Paste

8 OUNCES BLACK OLIVES, PITTED (ABOUT 6 OUNCES)

2 TABLESPOONS CAPERS, STRAINED AND RINSED

1 GARLIC CLOVE, MINCED

3 ANCHOVY FILLETS, CHOPPED

2 TABLESPOONS LEMON JUICE

FRESHLY GROUND BLACK PEPPER

ABOUT 2 TABLESPOONS OLIVE OIL

1 TABLESPOON FINELY CHOPPED TARRAGON OR FLAT-LEAVED PARSLEY

SERVES *6-8*

PREPARATION *10 minutes, plus chilling*

Calories per serving *67*
Total fat *High*
Saturated fat *Medium*
Protein *Low*
Carbohydrate *Low*
Cholesterol *None*
Vitamins *B12, E*
Minerals *Iron*

1 Place all the ingredients except oil and herbs in a food processor and blend until smooth.
2 With the machine still running, slowly add the olive oil. When 2 tablespoons have been added, taste and add a little more if necessary for a spreading consistency. Cover and chill.
3 Serve chilled, with the herbs sprinkled on top, and accompanied by warm toast.

Tyropitakia Lefteritsas

ROAST PEPPERS WITH ANCHOVY VINAIGRETTE

This is an improvisation of mine that became an instant success. The salty edge of the anchovies brings out the sweetness of the peppers. If you don't like strong tastes, however, reduce the number of anchovies in the dressing.

SERVES *4-6*

PREPARATION *about 15 minutes*

COOKING *40 minutes, plus cooling*

Calories per serving *111*
Total fat *High*
Saturated fat *Low*
Protein *Low*
Carbohydrate *Low*
Cholesterol *None*
Vitamins *A, B₃, B₆, B₁₂, Folate, C, E*
Minerals *Iron, Potassium*

6 RED BELL PEPPERS, OR A MIX OF RED AND YELLOW
FRESHLY GROUND BLACK PEPPER
2 TABLESPOONS CHOPPED OR WHOLE SMALL PURPLE BASIL LEAVES, TO GARNISH
1 LEMON CUT INTO WEDGES, TO SERVE

FOR THE ANCHOVY VINAIGRETTE:
4 CANNED OR BOTTLED ANCHOVIES, DRAINED AND COARSELY CHOPPED
1 GARLIC CLOVE, CHOPPED
JUICE OF 1 SMALL LEMON
2 TABLESPOONS OLIVE OIL

1 Preheat the oven to 375°F and cover a baking sheet with foil.

2 Place the peppers on the prepared baking sheet and bake for 40 minutes. Turn them over once after 20 minutes.

3 Take the peppers out of the oven and, when they are cool enough to handle, peel them. Then halve them, trim off the tops, and remove the seeds. Place the halves on a plate, outsides up, in a circle and set them aside. (This can be done the day before, but the peppers should then be covered with plastic wrap to prevent them from drying out.)

4 Make the anchovy vinaigrette: place the anchovies, garlic, and lemon juice in a blender or food processor and blend briefly. With the machine still running, add the oil in a steady stream and blend until well amalgamated into a runny velvety sauce.

5 Pour this dressing over the peppers, garnish with the basil leaves, and season with some freshly ground black pepper. It can now wait for 1 or 2 hours before serving. Serve with lemon wedges.

Roast Peppers with Anchovy Vinaigrette

CROSTINI CON FUNGHI
Tuscan Mushroom Crostini

Probably the most famous part of Tuscan antipasti, crostini are slices of toasted bread layered with mouthwatering toppings. The most familiar are made with chicken livers or black olives and anchovies.

1½ OUNCES DRIED FUNGHI PORCINI

5 OUNCES BUTTON MUSHROOMS

2 TABLESPOONS OLIVE OIL

2 SHALLOTS, PEELED AND FINELY CHOPPED

2 GARLIC CLOVES, PEELED AND CRUSHED

1 TEASPOON BRANDY

½ TEASPOON DRIED OREGANO

1 FRENCH BAGUETTE, CUT INTO THIN SLICES

SALT AND FRESHLY GROUND BLACK PEPPER

SERVES *4*

PREPARATION *about 15 minutes, plus 20 minutes' soaking*

COOKING *about 25 minutes*

Calories per serving *357*
Total fat *High*
Saturated fat *Medium*
Protein *Low*
Carbohydrate *Low*
Cholesterol *None*
Vitamins *B₁, B₂, B₃, B₆, Folate, E*
Minerals *Calcium, Potassium, Iron, Zinc, Selenium*

1 Soak the dried mushrooms in a bowl of warm water for about 20 minutes. Lift them out carefully in order not to disturb the grit at the bottom of the bowl. Place them in another bowl and rinse a few times until the water appears clear of grit. Pat them dry and chop coarsely. Pour the original soaking water through a muslin- or paper-towel-lined sieve and reserve.

2 Heat the olive oil in a wide-based pan and sauté the chopped shallots until translucent. Add the crushed garlic and then the reconstituted mushrooms with ⅔ cup of the strained soaking liquid, the brandy, and the dried oregano. Cover and simmer gently for 15 minutes.

3 In the meantime, wipe the fresh mushrooms and chop them coarsely. Turn the heat up, add them to the pan, and cook briskly for 5-7 minutes uncovered, stirring occasionally until most of the liquid they produce has evaporated. Season to taste.

4 When the contents of the pan have cooled, put them in a food processor and process them very briefly—they should be just chopped and not puréed. You can prepare the topping mixture up to this point in advance and keep it in the refrigerator.

5 Toast the slices of French bread.Spread a generous layer of the chopped mushroom mixture on top of each slice and serve immediately. The crostini can also be served just warm or even cold.

BRUSCHETTA TOSCANA
Grilled Tuscan Bread with Olives

SERVES *4*

PREPARATION *about 20 minutes*

COOKING *about 5 minutes*

Bruschetta, *in its simplicity, is one of those culinary items at the heart of a culture. It originated in Rome—according to Marcella Hazan its name is derived from* bruscare, *which means "to roast over coals"—and originally it was nothing more than toasted bread sprinkled with thick green olive oil.*

3 RIPE TOMATOES (ABOUT 8 OUNCES)

6 OUNCES BLACK OLIVES

2 CANNED SALTED ANCHOVIES

1 TABLESPOON LEMON JUICE

4 LARGE SLICES OF FRESH CRUSTY BREAD, ABOUT ½ INCH THICK

3 GARLIC CLOVES, PEELED AND ROUGHLY CRUSHED WITH THE FLAT OF A KNIFE

2 TABLESPOONS OLIVE OIL

FRESHLY GROUND BLACK PEPPER

1 TABLESPOON FINELY CHOPPED BASIL LEAVES

Calories per serving *283*
Total fat *High*
Saturated fat *Low*
Protein *Low*
Carbohydrate *Low*
Cholesterol *None*
Vitamins *B₁, B₃, B₆, B₁₂, Folate, E*
Minerals *Calcium, Iron, Selenium, Potassium*

1 Blanch, skin, quarter, and deseed the tomatoes. Set them aside. Pit the olives and place them with the anchovies and lemon juice in a food processor. Process rapidly for a few seconds until the mixture resembles breadcrumbs. Add the tomatoes and process rapidly for a few more seconds.

2 Toast the bread on both sides until crisp and golden and rub one side of each slice with the crushed garlic. Cut the slices in half to make them easier to handle. Dribble a little oil on the garlicky side and then add a thin—or thick, according to taste—layer of the olive and tomato mixture, some pepper, and finally a little fresh basil. Serve immediately.

GRILLED HALOUMI ON ARUGULA

Cypriot haloumi cheese, with its elastic texture, is totally transformed when grilled. The real secret is to soak it in water for 30 minutes and then rinse it under cold running water to extract its saltiness. In the winter, when outdoor grilling is difficult, I use a heavy ridged cast-iron grill pan and the results are wonderful. The cheese should be served immediately, otherwise it becomes leathery.

1 HALOUMI CHEESE (ABOUT 6 OUNCES), SOAKED IN COLD WATER FOR 30 MINUTES AND RINSED

1 TABLESPOON OLIVE OIL

4 OUNCES ARUGULA, COARSELY CHOPPED

1 POMEGRANATE, PEELED AND SEEDS EXTRACTED (OPTIONAL WHEN OUT OF SEASON)

1 TABLESPOON VEGETABLE OIL

FOR THE DRESSING:

2 TABLESPOONS OLIVE OIL

1 TABLESPOON BALSAMIC VINEGAR

SALT AND FRESHLY GROUND PEPPER

SERVES *4*

PREPARATION *about 15 minutes, plus 30 minutes' soaking*

COOKING *about 5 minutes*

Calories per serving *229*
Total fat *High*
Saturated fat *High*
Protein *Low*
Carbohydrate *Low*
Cholesterol *30 mg*
Vitamins *A, B₁₂, E*
Minerals *Calcium, Potassium, Iron, Zinc*

1 Pat the cheese dry and slice it into 5-6 medium slices. Coat with olive oil and set aside. Spread the arugula on a small platter and scatter pomegranate seeds over it.

2 Oil a cast-iron grill pan lightly with the vegetable oil and heat it until quite hot, but not smoking. Place the cheese slices on it and don't move them. Let them cook for a couple of minutes and then turn them over. Let them cook for 1-2 more minutes. Lift them and place them directly on the salad in a circle or fan shape.

3 While the cheese is cooking, beat the dressing ingredients lightly in a bowl and season to taste. Dribble the dressing over cheese and salad and serve immediately.

ANDALUSIAN GAZPACHO

"Reapers and agricultural labourers could never stand the sun's fire without this cooling acetous diet.
This was the oxikratos *of the Greeks, the* posca, *potable food, meat and drink,* potus et esca, *which*
formed part of the rations of the Roman soldiers…" wrote Richard Ford in his Gatherings from Spain,
published in 1846. And he was right. In the midday heat of August, this makes a perfect lunch.

2 SLICES OF STALE BREAD, CRUSTS REMOVED

2 POUNDS RIPE TOMATOES, SKINNED AND CHOPPED

1 FRESH GREEN CHILI, DESEEDED AND CHOPPED

3-INCH LENGTH OF CUCUMBER, PEELED AND
COARSELY CHOPPED

2 GARLIC CLOVES, PEELED AND CRUSHED

½ GREEN OR RED BELL PEPPER, DESEEDED AND
CHOPPED

2 TABLESPOONS OLIVE OIL

2 TABLESPOONS RED WINE VINEGAR

½ TEASPOON PAPRIKA

2 TABLESPOONS PARSLEY, CHOPPED

7-8 BASIL OR MINT LEAVES

SALT AND FRESHLY GROUND BLACK PEPPER

TO GARNISH:

LARGE HANDFUL OF BASIL, TORN INTO STRIPS

1 GREEN OR RED BELL PEPPER, TRIMMED, DESEEDED
AND FINELY DICED

1½-INCH CUCUMBER, PEELED AND FINELY DICED

3 TABLESPOONS FINELY DICED RED ONION

GARLIC CROUTONS

SERVES 6

PREPARATION *about*
25 minutes, plus 10
minutes' soaking and
2-3 hours' chilling

Calories per serving *130*
Total fat *Medium*
Saturated fat *Low*
Protein *Low*
Carbohydrate *Medium*
Cholesterol *None*
Vitamins *A, B₁, B₃, B₆,*
Folate, E
Minerals *Potassium, Iron*

1 Soak the bread in water for 10 minutes, squeeze it a little, and place in a food processor or blender with the remaining ingredients and 1¼ cups water. If the chili is very hot, add only half. Process until smooth. Taste and adjust the seasoning. If you like a sharper taste add a little more vinegar.

2 Empty into a bowl, cover, and chill for 2-3 hours or longer.

3 Before serving the soup, float 2-3 ice cubes in it to keep it chilled and, if needed, dilute it with a little more iced water. Serve the garnishes in separate small bowls and let people help themselves.

TURKISH COLD YOGURT SOUP

The Turks are supposed to have brought yogurt with them to Europe, and they certainly display a
preference for it. It is used in soups, served with poached eggs in cilbir, *spread over fried vegetables, used*
in salads with spinach or purslane, used to marinate kebabs, made into a cold drink called ayran, *and it*
features in cacik, *the Turkish Yogurt and Cucumber Salad (see page 40). This refreshing soup is identical*
to cacik, *except for the volume of ingredients. Proceed as for the* cacik *recipe, but add half the measured*
ingredients again and dilute with ⅔ cup cold water, or a little more to taste. As well as the fresh mint,
add also 2 tablespoons of finely chopped fresh dill. Serve chilled.

SERVES 4-6

PREPARATION *15*
minutes, plus chilling

Calories per serving *76*
Total fat *High*
Saturated fat *Low*
Protein *High*
Carbohydrate *Low*
Cholesterol *3 mg*
Vitamins *B₂, B₃*
Minerals *Calcium, Iodine*

Andalusian Gazpacho

SOUPE AU PISTOU

This is not unlike Italian minestrone, *but it becomes intoxicating with the addition of the fragrant* pistou. *Its ingredients vary according to seasonal availability, so one can loosely improvise. A few years ago, for instance, I had a delicious version in Nice in the early summer, where everything used in the soup was green—fresh fava beans, peas, green beans and zucchini.*

Pistou is like Pesto (page 33) without the pine nuts. It is mixed into the soup just before it is served, and I offer an extra bowl of it along with a bowl of grated Parmesan cheese on the table.

SERVES 6

PREPARATION *about 25 minutes, plus overnight soaking*

COOKING *about 50 minutes*

Calories per serving *300*
Total fat *High*
Saturated fat *High*
Protein *High*
Carbohydrate *Low*
Cholesterol *31 mg*
Vitamins *A, B group, E*
Minerals *Calcium, Iron, Zinc, Potassium*

3 DRIED HARICOT BEANS, SOAKED OVERNIGHT
2 TABLESPOONS OLIVE OIL
1 MEDIUM ONION, PEELED AND THINLY SLICED
2 LEEKS, FINELY CHOPPED
1 POUND TOMATOES, SKINNED AND CHOPPED
2 SMALL POTATOES, DICED
10 OUNCES ZUCCHINI, DICED
2 SMALL CARROTS, DICED
5 OUNCES GREEN BEANS, EACH CUT INTO 3-4 PIECES
6 CUPS HOT WATER
LARGE HANDFUL OF FLAT-LEAVED PARSLEY, CHOPPED
SMALL BUNCH OF CHERVIL, CHOPPED

2 OUNCES SPAGHETTINI, BROKEN INTO SHORT PIECES
SALT AND FRESHLY GROUND BLACK PEPPER
1 CUP FRESHLY GRATED PARMESAN TO SERVE

FOR THE PISTOU:
4 OUNCES BASIL LEAVES
2 LARGE GARLIC CLOVES, MINCED
4 TABLESPOONS OLIVE OIL
½ CUP PARMESAN CHEESE, FRESHLY GRATED
2 TABLESPOONS FRESHLY GRATED PECORINO SARDO OR ROMANO CHEESE

1 Rinse the haricot beans, cover with water, and boil for about 30 minutes until soft. Strain and discard the liquid.

2 Heat the oil in a large saucepan, add the onion, and sauté until glistening. Add the leeks and 1-2 minutes later, add the remaining vegetables, including the boiled beans. Turn the vegetables, with a spatula for 3-4 minutes to coat them in the oil.

3 Add the hot water with the herbs and seasoning to taste. Cover and simmer for 40 minutes.

4 While the soup is simmering, make the pistou: place all the ingredients apart from the cheeses in a food processor and give it a quick burst. Stop and scrape everything down, then do it again. If the mixture appears too dry, add 1 tablespoon of water. When it has a creamy appearance, add the cheeses and give it one more rapid burst. Just before using, dilute a little by adding 2 tablespoons of warm water.

5 About 20 minutes before the soup is to be served, bring it back to the boil. Add the pasta and simmer for 8-10 minutes. Remove the soup from the heat, mix in 3-4 tablespoons of pistou, and serve. Offer the remaining pistou and the Parmesan in bowls.

Soupe au Pistou

ZUPPA DI CECI
Chickpea Soup

Chickpeas have a wonderfully nutty flavor that makes them the ideal warming winter staple. Each Mediterranean country has its own chickpea soup: in Italy it is zuppa di ceci, *in Greece it is* revythia soupa, *in Turkey there is* nohut çorbasi, *in Languedoc in France there is* soupe aux pois chiches. *The variations are endless, and in Tuscany this particularly delicious soup is on every restaurant menu.*

Chickpeas are, of course, a wonderful cupboard ingredient, but they do have to be soaked in water overnight. A pressure cooker is ideal for cooking this dish.

SERVES *4*

PREPARATION *15-20 minutes, plus overnight soaking*

COOKING *about 1 hour if using a pressure cooker, otherwise about 2¼ hours*

Calories per serving *380*
Total fat *Medium*
Saturated fat *Low*
Protein *Medium*
Carbohydrate *Medium*
Cholesterol *None*
Vitamins *B₁, B₂, B₃, B₆, Folate, E*
Minerals *Calcium, Potassium, Iron, Zinc, Selenium*

8 OUNCES CHICKPEAS, PICKED CLEAN AND SOAKED OVERNIGHT
3 TABLESPOONS OLIVE OIL
1 CELERY STALK WITH LEAVES, FINELY CHOPPED
SMALL SPRIG OF FRESH ROSEMARY, FINELY CHOPPED
6-7 FRESH SAGE LEAVES, FINELY CHOPPED, PLUS A FEW MORE WHOLE LEAVES FOR GARNISH (OPTIONAL)
4 GARLIC CLOVES, PEELED AND CRUSHED
1 SMALL CAN (7-OUNCES) OF CHOPPED TOMATOES
JUICE OF ½ LEMON
SALT AND FRESHLY GROUND BLACK PEPPER

TO SERVE:
4 SMALL SLICES OF BREAD
2 GARLIC CLOVES, PEELED AND SLICED IN HALF LENGTHWISE

1 Rinse and drain the chickpeas. Place them in a pressure cooker, cover them with fresh water by at least 1 inch and bring to a boil. Skim the white froth that rises to the surface until clear. Cover, weight, and cook for about 15-20 minutes under full pressure. If using an ordinary saucepan, allow at least 1½ hours until the chickpeas are soft.

2 Drain, reserving the liquid. Take 2 cupfuls of chickpeas and purée them with 2 cups of the reserved liquid. Set aside.

3 Heat the oil in the same saucepan and add the celery and herbs. A minute later add the garlic. As soon as the garlic becomes aromatic add the chopped tomatoes and sauté together for a few minutes. Add the remaining chick-peas and stir to coat them in the sauce for 3-4 minutes. Add at least 1¼ cups of the reserved liquid (if there is not enough, add a little water) with some seasoning. Cover and simmer for 20 minutes.

4 Stir in the puréed chickpeas with their liquid, cover, and simmer for 15 more minutes, stirring often as it may stick.

5 Add the lemon juice and, if necessary, dilute the soup to the desired consistency with a little more hot water. Adjust the seasoning.

6 Just before serving, toast the bread. While it is still hot, rub its surface with the garlic. Place a slice of bread in each soup bowl and pour the soup on top. Garnish with a few more sage leaves, if you wish.

Zuppa di Ceci

PASTA E FAGIOLI
Borlotti Bean and Pasta Soup

This is a great Tuscan peasant dish that is both substantial and soul-warming. There are countless versions of it, using all kinds of beans. I have had it in Venice with borlotti beans, and I have made it with beautiful beans called pavone—peacocks—*that I bought in the Rialto market. These were large and plump and were adorned with pink hues, like Venetian marbling. In addition to their pretty looks they had a very enticing taste.*

SERVES *4-6*

PREPARATION *about 20 minutes, plus overnight soaking*

COOKING *about 1¼ hours*

Calories per serving *376*
Total fat *Medium*
Saturated fat *Medium*
Protein *High*
Carbohydrate *Low*
Cholesterol *24 mg*
Vitamins *A, B group*
Minerals *Calcium, Potassium, Iron, Zinc*

10 OUNCES BORLOTTI OR CRANBERRY BEANS, PICKED CLEAN AND SOAKED OVERNIGHT
1 LARGE CARROT, DICED
3 TABLESPOONS OLIVE OIL
1 MEDIUM ONION, THINLY SLICED

2 OUNCES PANCETTA, SLICED IN FINE STRIPS
3 OUNCES SMALL TUBULAR PASTA
2 OUNCES FRESHLY GRATED PARMESAN CHEESE
SALT AND FRESHLY GROUND BLACK PEPPER

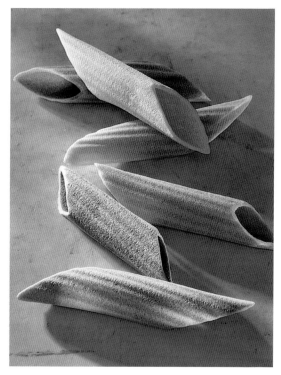

1 Rinse the beans, place them in a saucepan and cover with 6 cups of water. Bring to a boil and skim. Add the carrot, cover, and cook gently for about 40-50 minutes, until the beans are tender.

2 Take out half of the beans and mash them in a food processor with some of the cooking liquid. Empty them back into the pot and mix well.

3 Half an hour before it is to be served, finish the dish: heat the oil gently in a frying pan and sauté the onion until it starts to turn light golden. Turn up the heat a little, add the pancetta, and sauté until crisp. Mix this into the beans, season to taste, and bring back to a boil. The soup should be quite creamy, but if too thick dilute with a little hot water.

4 Add the pasta and simmer gently for 6-7 minutes, stirring often as it may stick.

5 Off the heat, mix in half of the Parmesan and serve. Offer a bowl with the remaining Parmesan and some crusty bread.

KOTOPOULO SOUPA AVGOLEMONO
Chicken Soup with Egg-and-Lemon Sauce

This very delicious soup could be served either as a first course or as a meal in itself for an informal occasion or a family lunch.

1 STEWING CHICKEN OR BOILING FOWL, WEIGHING ABOUT 3½ POUNDS

1 ONION, PEELED AND SLICED IN HALF

2 CARROTS

2 CELERY STALKS, EACH TRIMMED AND SLICED INTO 3-4 PIECES

SMALL HANDFUL OF PARSLEY

3-4 BLACK PEPPERCORNS

SALT

¼ CUP SHORT-GRAIN RICE

1 RECIPE EGG-AND-LEMON SAUCE (PAGE 36)

LEMON QUARTERS, TO SERVE

SERVES *6*

PREPARATION *10-15 minutes*

COOKING *about 1½ hours, plus cooling*

Calories per serving *150*
Total fat *Low*
Saturated fat *Low*
Protein *High*
Carbohydrate *Low*
Cholesterol *118 mg*
Vitamins *A, B group*
Minerals *Zinc, Potassium, Selenium, Iodine*

1 Rinse the chicken, place it in a large saucepan, and cover with 7½ cups water. Bring to a boil and skim until clear.

2 Add all the vegetables, the parsley, peppercorns, and salt to taste. Cover and cook for about 1 hour, or 30 minutes longer if a boiling fowl is used. When the leg of the bird can be pulled easily away from the body, it is done. Take the chicken out, strain the broth and discard the vegetables.

3 Pull away the two breast halves from the bird, skin them, and discard the skin. Dice the meat. You can do the same with the leg meat if you want the soup to be more substantial, otherwise keep the legs—for a salad, perhaps.

4 Pour the broth back into the saucepan and add the breast meat. It can be prepared up to this stage well in advance, even the day before.

5 About a quarter of an hour before the soup is to be served, bring it back to the boil and add the rice. Cover and cook for about 8 minutes. Let it cool off the heat for 5 minutes.

6 Make the sauce while the soup is cooling: slowly add a ladleful of chicken broth to the egg mixture and beat together for 1 minute, then add another ladleful and beat. By now the sauce will be warm, so you can pour it slowly into the soup, off the heat, and stir vigorously to mix.

7 Warm the soup up over a very, very gentle heat—otherwise the eggs may cook, although the cornstarch will safeguard against that.

8 Serve immediately, with a plate of lemon quarters and fresh bread on the table.

Pasta, Rice & Grains

CHARD CANNELLONI WITH PINE NUTS

When I first went to Rome in 1962 the two dishes that impressed me most were spaghetti alle vongole and cannelloni. I remember buying squares of fresh pasta and taking them back home to my mother in Athens in order to recreate cannelloni. For this vegetarian version I use Swiss chard—which has a sweeter taste than spinach, and an aroma that reminds me of the open fields—a number of different cheeses and pine nuts, or occasionally coarsely chopped walnuts for a different texture.

SERVES 6

PREPARATION
40 minutes

COOKING
about 1 hour

Calories per serving *718*
Total fat *High*
Saturated fat *High*
Protein *Medium*
Carbohydrate *Low*
Cholesterol *157 mg*
Vitamins *A, B group, C, E*
Minerals *Calcium,
Potassium, Iron, Zinc,
Selenium, Iodine*

2¼ POUNDS SWISS CHARD, OR 2 POUNDS FRESH SPINACH, OR 9 OUNCES FROZEN LEAF SPINACH, THAWED

2 TABLESPOONS OLIVE OIL

1 MEDIUM ONION, FINELY CHOPPED

LARGE HANDFUL OF BASIL, LEAVES AND STALKS, CHOPPED

1 EGG

6 OUNCES FRESH RICOTTA CHEESE

1 CUP FRESHLY GRATED PARMESAN CHEESE

1 CUP FRESHLY GRATED PECORINO CHEESE

½ CUP PINE NUTS, TOASTED LIGHTLY

4½ CUPS BÉCHAMEL SAUCE (PAGE 36)

24 QUICK-COOK DRIED CANNELLONI TUBES (ABOUT 12 OUNCES)

PEPPER

1 If using chard or larger older spinach leaves, trim off and discard the thick stalks. Fill the sink with water and soak the leaves for 10 minutes in order to dislodge any grit. Lift the leaves out by hand and repeat the process until the water appears clear. Put the leaves in a large saucepan with a little salt, cover, and cook gently for 10-15 minutes, stirring occasionally and making sure they don't dry out. Drain through a colander and gently squeeze out excess moisture (carefully, as it will still be quite hot). Chop the leaves coarsely. If using thawed frozen spinach, just squeeze out the moisture and chop.

2 Preheat the oven 350°F and lightly oil one large or two medium-sized ovenproof dishes that can be brought from the oven straight to the table. Heat the remaining oil gently in a frying pan and sauté the onion until glistening. Add the chopped chard or spinach leaves and the basil and sauté together for 3-4 minutes. Let this cool a little.

3 Beat the egg lightly in a large bowl, add the ricotta and, using a fork, mix it with the egg. Add two-thirds of the Parmesan and all of the Pecorino, the sautéed leaves, the pine nuts, and 3 tablespoons of the béchamel. The stuffing should be of a thick creamy consistency, but not solid. Season with pepper.

4 Stuff the cannelloni with the filling, using a small spoon or knife and pushing the stuffing down with a chopstick or a skewer. Place the stuffed cannelloni tightly together in a single layer in the prepared dish(es) and spread the remaining béchamel sauce evenly over them. Sprinkle the top with the remaining Parmesan and bake for 40-45 minutes, until the top is golden and the cannelloni properly cooked.

Chard Cannelloni with Pine Nuts

PENNE CON SALSA CRUDA
Penne with Raw Tomato Sauce

This very refreshing and light dish should be made at the height of summer when the weather is hot and tomatoes are sugary. Our friend Guido Jesurum introduced us to it back in 1972, in his lovely house overlooking Mount Etna on the Aeolian island of Salina.

14 OUNCES PENNE RIGATE OR OTHER PASTA
1 TABLESPOON OLIVE OIL
SALT AND FRESHLY GROUND BLACK PEPPER
FRESHLY GRATED PARMESAN CHEESE, TO SERVE

FOR THE SALSA CRUDA:
1½ POUNDS LARGE RIPE TOMATOES
2 GARLIC CLOVES, PEELED AND CRUSHED
2 TABLESPOONS OLIVE OIL
1 TABLESPOON GOOD-QUALITY CAPERS, RINSED
LARGE HANDFUL OF BASIL, SHREDDED BY HAND

SERVES *4*

PREPARATION *about 10 minutes*

COOKING *10-15 minutes, depending on the pasta*

Calories per serving *849*
Total fat *Low*
Saturated fat *Low*
Protein *Low*
Carbohydrate *High*
Cholesterol *10 mg*
Vitamins *A, B group, C, E*
Minerals *Calcium, Potassium, Iron, Zinc, Selenium*

1 First prepare the tomatoes for the sauce: skin them and, holding them from the stem end, grate them coarsely. Alternatively, peel them, trim off their stalks, place in a food processor, and process rapidly to achieve a coarse consistency. Put the grated or processed tomatoes in a bowl, cover, and keep refrigerated if they are not to be used immediately.

2 Cook the pasta: bring a large pan of lightly salted water to the boil, add ½ tablespoon of the olive oil and cook the pasta in it until just al dente—tender but still firm. Drain and mix with the remaining oil.

3 Just before the dish is to be served, mix the tomatoes with the remaining sauce ingredients and season with pepper. Pour over the pasta and toss.

4 Serve immediately, with a bowl of grated Parmesan served separately.

PENNE WITH SUN-DRIED TOMATOES AND MOZZARELLA

This easy dish is quite delicious, with the mozzarella cubes mellowing the robustness of the sun-dried tomatoes. The sauce has to be prepared very rapidly, 5-7 minutes in total, and must be consumed immediately, before the mozzarella becomes leathery. Other pasta shapes, such as fusilli, farfalle or orecchiette, can be used instead of the penne.

14 OUNCES PENNE

6-8 SUN-DRIED TOMATO HALVES IN OIL, CHOPPED

3 TABLESPOONS OLIVE OIL

3 GARLIC CLOVES, PEELED AND CRUSHED

12 OUNCES CHERRY TOMATOES

4 LARGE SPRIGS OF FRESH BASIL (INCLUDING STEMS), TORN BY HAND

SALT AND FRESHLY GROUND BLACK PEPPER

5 OUNCES BUFFALO MOZZARELLA CHEESE, CUT INTO ¾-INCH DICE

FRESHLY GRATED PARMESAN CHEESE, TO SERVE

1 Boil the pasta in plenty of lightly salted water until just al dente. Drain and keep warm.

2 Heat the oil in the same saucepan, and add the sun-dried tomatoes and garlic. As soon as the garlic becomes aromatic, add the whole cherry tomatoes and roll them around with a wooden spatula over gentle heat for just 1 minute to coat them in the oil. The cherry tomatoes should still be intact.

3 Add the pasta, the basil, and a generous sprinkling of pepper. Toss for 1-2 minutes to mix with the tomatoes and garlic. Add the mozzarella, mix it in quickly, and allow it just to warm through. Remove the pan from the heat before the cheese starts to melt and become sticky. Serve immediately, with freshly grated Parmesan.

SERVES *4 as a main course, or 6 as a first course*

PREPARATION *10 minutes*

COOKING *15-20 minutes, depending on the pasta*

Calories per serving *641*
Total fat *Medium*
Saturated fat *Medium*
Protein *Low*
Carbohydrate *Low*
Cholesterol *23 mg*
Vitamins *A, B group, C, E*
Minerals *Calcium, Potassium, Iron, Zinc, Selenium*

Overleaf, left to right: Conchiglie with Seafood (page 70),
Penne with Sun-Dried Tomatoes and Mozzarella, Spaghetti alle Vongole (page 71)

SPAGHETTI CON LE ACCIUGHE
Spaghetti with Anchovy and Caper Sauce

This is our family's favorite sauce when we are in our house in the Aegean island of Alonnisos in the summer. Although the sauce has a strong piquant taste, once it has coated the pasta it loses its forcefulness and becomes quite tame. It is quick and easy to prepare and everyone loves it.

SERVES *4*

PREPARATION *10 minutes*

COOKING *about 30 minutes*

Calories per serving *468*
Total fat *Low*
Saturated fat *Low*
Protein *Low*
Carbohydrate *High*
Cholesterol *None*
Vitamins *B group, C*
Minerals *Iron, Zinc, Potassium*

2-3 TABLESPOONS OLIVE OIL
2 LARGE ONIONS, ABOUT 12 OUNCES, PEELED AND THINLY SLICED
1-2 GREEN CHILIES, DESEEDED AND FINELY CHOPPED
3 GARLIC CLOVES, PEELED AND CRUSHED
1½ TABLESPOONS CAPERS, RINSED AND DRAINED

2-OUNCE CAN OF ANCHOVIES IN OIL, DRAINED AND CHOPPED
10 BLACK OLIVES
2 TABLESPOONS FINELY CHOPPED PARSLEY
FRESHLY GROUND BLACK PEPPER
14 OUNCES SPAGHETTI OR LINGUINE

1 Heat the oil gently in a medium-sized saucepan and add the onions. Stir to coat them in the oil and cook until they become translucent, about 4-5 minutes.
2 Add the chili(es) and stir together for 1-2 minutes to allow them to release their oils and aroma. Then immediately stir in the garlic and, as soon as its aroma rises—almost immediately—add ½ cup of water and simmer gently for 10 minutes.

3 Add the capers, anchovies, olives, parsley, and pepper, and simmer for 5 more minutes.
4 While the sauce is being prepared, cook the pasta in a large pan of lightly salted boiling water, drain, and keep some of the pasta water aside. Return the pasta to the pan and add the anchovy sauce and 2 tablespoons of the reserved pasta water. Toss gently to mix everything and coat the pasta in the sauce.

CONCHIGLIE WITH SEAFOOD

Conchiglie—sea shells—fits thematically with seafood, but any pasta with cavities, such as fusilli, penne, or the Apulian orecchiette (little ears) will do. Mussels are indispensable to the dish, as they add an unparalleled flavor of the sea. (See previous pages.)

SERVES *4 as a main course, or 6 as a first course*

PREPARATION *20-25 minutes*

COOKING *40-45 minutes, depending on the pasta*

1½ POUNDS FRESH MUSSELS, PREPARED AS ON PAGE 93
⅔ CUP WHITE WINE
1 POUND 2 OUNCES SQUID, PREPARED AS ON PAGE 75
3 TABLESPOONS OLIVE OIL
1 LARGE ONION, FINELY CHOPPED

3 GARLIC CLOVES, PEELED AND CHOPPED
2-3 SPRIGS OF FRESH OREGANO, CHOPPED
SALT AND FRESHLY GROUND BLACK PEPPER
3-4 SPRIGS OF BASIL, TORN BY HAND
6 OUNCES COOKED PEELED SHRIMP
14 OUNCES CONCHIGLIE

1 Place the mussels in a large saucepan with the wine. Cover and boil briskly for 5 minutes or until they open, shaking the pan vigorously from time to time. Let them cool a little.
2 Using a slotted spoon, lift the mussels out and transfer to a bowl. Let the liquid settle so that the grit sinks. Discard any mussels which remain closed. Take most out of their shells and place them in another bowl, but leave a few in their shells for visual effect. To keep the mussels moist, strain their liquor over them through a fine sieve lined with paper towels.
3 The squid bodies should be kept intact, rinsed inside and out, and then sliced into thin rings; divide the tentacles into 3-4 pieces.
4 Heat the oil gently in a large pan and sauté the onion until lightly golden. Add the garlic. When it is aromatic, add the squid and sauté for 10-15 minutes, until all moisture evaporates.
5 Add most of the strained mussel liquid, the oregano, salt and pepper. Cover and cook gently for 15-20 minutes, until the squid is just tender. If needed, add a little hot water. Add the shrimp and cook for 2-3 minutes. Mix in the mussels and basil and remove from heat.
6 While the squid is cooking, cook the pasta in plenty of boiling water until al dente. Drain and mix into the seafood mixture. Serve.

Calories per serving *526*
Total fat *Low*
Saturated fat *Low*
Protein *High*
Carbohydrate *Low*
Cholesterol *345 mg*
Vitamins *B group, E*
Minerals *Calcium, Potassium, Iodine, Selenium, Iron, Zinc*

SPAGHETTI ALLE VONGOLE
Spaghetti with Clams and Garlic

Small white Mediterranean clams appear occasionally at fishmongers and are cheap. (See pages 68-9.)

10 OUNCES SPAGHETTI
2½ POUNDS CLAMS
2-3 GARLIC CLOVES, PEELED AND CRUSHED
3 TABLESPOONS GOOD OLIVE OIL

3 SCALLIONS, THINLY SLICED
3 TABLESPOONS FINELY CHOPPED PARSLEY
3 TABLESPOONS FINELY CHOPPED FRESH DILL
SALT AND FRESHLY GROUND BLACK PEPPER

1 Place the clams in a large bowl of cold water and let their grit sink. Lift out and repeat the process until water is perfectly clear. Discard any that remain open when they are tapped.
2 Heat the oil in a large frying pan and sauté the scallions gently in it without allowing them to brown. Add the garlic and parsley and sauté briefly until aromatic.
3 Turn the heat up, add the clams, and stir continuously for 2-3 minutes to coat them in the oil. Remove the pan from heat and let the clams stand briefly until slightly cooler.
4 Working quickly, pick half the clams out of their shells and discard the shells. (Discard any that have not opened during cooking.)
5 While the clams are cooking, boil the spaghetti in plenty of lightly salted water for about 8 minutes, making sure it is not overcooked. Drain, reserving a cup of liquid.
6 Heat the clams up again if necessary, stirring continuously. Add salt and pepper, the dill, 2-3 tablespoons of the reserved liquid, and the pasta. Mix well over gentle heat for a few seconds to coat the pasta and serve.

SERVES *2 as main course, or 4 as a first course*

PREPARATION *about 20 minutes*

COOKING *about 15 minutes*

Calories per serving *450*
Total fat *Low*
Saturated fat *Low*
Protein *High*
Carbohydrate *High*
Cholesterol *112 mg*
Vitamins *A, B group*
Minerals *Calcium, Potassium, Iron, Zinc, Iodine*

ASPARAGUS RISOTTO

This is a risotto with a very refined taste and elegant looks, making it perfect for a summer lunch or an al fresco dinner. It is best to make the stock beforehand, so the dish is not too laborious on the day. Allow about ½ cup arborio, carnaroli or vialone nano rice per person. Remember that a risotto must be cooked and consumed immediately, while it is still smooth and creamy. A crisp, green salad and fresh bread are the perfect accompaniment to this dish.

SERVES *4-5*

PREPARATION *about 20 minutes*

COOKING *40-45 minutes*

Calories per serving *454*
Total fat *Low*
Saturated fat *Medium*
Protein *Low*
Carbohydrate *High*
Cholesterol *22 mg*
Vitamins *A, B group, C, E*
Minerals *Calcium, Potassium, Iron, Zinc, Selenium, Iodine*

14 OUNCES ASPARAGUS, TRIMMED OF HARD STEMS
3 TABLESPOONS LIGHT CREAM
LARGE HANDFUL OF BASIL LEAVES, ROUGHLY TORN
3 TABLESPOONS OLIVE OIL
1 MEDIUM ONION, PEELED AND FINELY CHOPPED
4-5 SCALLIONS, COARSELY CHOPPED

2 CUPS RISOTTO RICE
⅔ CUP DRY WHITE WINE
5 CUPS HOT CHICKEN OR BEEF STOCK, WITH FAT REMOVED
1 CUP GRATED PARMESAN CHEESE
SALT AND FRESHLY GROUND BLACK PEPPER

1 Cut off the asparagus tips and set aside. Cut each stalk into two and cook in plenty of lightly salted boiling water for 2 minutes. Remove from the pan with a slotted spoon and drain. Next drop the tips in the boiling water and boil very briefly, for 30 seconds only. Take out of the pan and drain separately.

2 Place just over half of the stalk pieces in a blender with the cream, a few basil leaves and stems, and 2-3 tablespoons of the asparagus cooking liquid. Blend to a light green velvety sauce and set aside. Chop the remaining stalk pieces into thin rounds.

3 Heat the oil in a heavy wide-based pan and sauté the onion and scallions in it until just wilted. Add the rice gradually, stirring over gentle heat until well coated in the oil. Add the wine and, once absorbed, start adding ladlefuls of the hot stock and ⅔ cup of the asparagus cooking liquid. Keep stirring to prevent the rice from sticking.

4 After about 25 minutes—when the rice has doubled its volume, is losing its chalky color, and is becoming soft—season to taste and add the puréed asparagus. Stir it gently into the risotto, which will turn a lovely pale green color. Simmer for 10 more minutes. Keep tasting the rice at this stage in order to catch it at the desired moment. It should be soft outside but firm in the middle. It should also have a very creamy appearance, so add more liquid if necessary.

5 Once the risotto is ready, add the remaining basil, half of the Parmesan, the asparagus stalk segments, and half of the tips. Mix gently, cover, and turn the heat off. It can now wait for 5 minutes but no more.

6 Empty on to a warm platter, scatter the remaining asparagus over the top, garnish with a few more basil leaves if you wish, and serve with a bowl of the remaining cheese.

Asparagus Risotto

LINGUINE CON PEPERONI ARROSTITI
Linguine with Roast Pepper Sauce

Inspired by a pasta dish with peperonade (sautéed pepper strips) served by my friend Henriette Valvini, this fresh approach to pasta uses a light sauce which, nevertheless, has a sophisticated taste. This treatment also suits other types of pastas, such as rigatoni, penne, or conchiglie.

For a rather rich addition, roast a respectable amount of whole garlic cloves—about 15—wrapped in foil in the oven with the peppers for 40 minutes, and then squeeze the delicious roast garlic pulp out of each clove over the pasta.

1 POUND LINGUINE

6 RED (OR A MIXTURE OF RED AND YELLOW) BELL PEPPERS, RINSED AND DRIED

2 TABLESPOONS OLIVE OIL

3 GARLIC CLOVES, FINELY CHOPPED

2 TABLESPOONS LIGHT CREAM OR LOW-FAT FRESH FARMER CHEESE

4-5 LARGE SPRIGS OF FRESH BASIL, TORN BY HAND

SALT AND FRESHLY GROUND BLACK PEPPER

15 WHOLE GARLIC CLOVES (OPTIONAL)

2 OUNCES PECORINO ROMANO OR PARMESAN CHEESE, FRESHLY GRATED, TO SERVE

SERVES *4-5*

PREPARATION *10-15 minutes*

COOKING *45-50 minutes*

Calories per serving *464*
Total fat *Low*
Saturated fat *Low*
Protein *Low*
Carbohydrate *Low*
Cholesterol *13 mg*
Vitamins *A, B group, C, E*
Minerals *Calcium, Potassium, Iron, Zinc, Selenium*

1 Preheat the oven to 375°F and line a baking sheet with foil. Place the peppers on the prepared baking sheet, leaving a little space between them, and roast for 30-35 minutes, turning them over once halfway.

2 Take the peppers out of the oven, let them cool a little, and then peel, discarding the tops, white pith, and seeds as you go. Slice the pepper flesh in thin strips and set aside.

3 Heat the oil in a large frying pan and sauté the garlic in it until aromatic. Add the peppers and sauté for 3-4 minutes to coat them in the oil and garlic. Season to taste and remove from the heat.

4 Place half of the pepper mixture in a food processor, add the cream or farmer cheese, and process until smooth.

5 Toward the end of the pepper cooking time, bring a large saucepan with plenty of water to the boil. Add a little salt and cook the pasta until just al dente. Drain, reserving a cupful of the liquid, and place the pasta back in the saucepan.

6 Dilute the smooth pepper sauce with 3 tablespoons of the cooking liquid and pour the light pink sauce over the pasta.

7 Heat the remaining peppers in the frying pan, add the basil, and toss around for a few seconds only until it looks a little wilted. Empty the contents of the pan into the pasta and toss with a fork to coat all the strands with the sauce. If it appears too dry, add a little more of the pasta liquid. If you have opted for the whole roast cloves of garlic, this is the moment to add the pulp by squeezing each clove onto the dish.

8 Serve immediately, with a bowl of cheese on the table.

RISOTTO NERO
Venetian Black Squid Risotto

Black squid risotto is a landmark of Venetian cuisine. The addition of the ink makes the risotto quite sweet, but if you don't like it black, discard the ink sacs. The squid casserole should be prepared in advance. The rice takes about 35-40 minutes, and it can be cooked while people are having their first course. It must then be consumed immediately. An absolute must for its taste is the fish stock, which can be made from bones and heads.

1¾ POUNDS LARGE SQUID

2 TABLESPOONS OLIVE OIL

2 MEDIUM ONIONS, SLICED

1 GLASS OF DRY WHITE WINE

SALT AND FRESHLY GROUND BLACK PEPPER

FOR THE RISOTTO:

3-4 SHALLOTS, THINLY SLICED

4 SCALLIONS, THICKLY SLICED

2 TABLESPOONS OLIVE OIL

2 CUPS ARBORIO OR VIALONE NANO RICE

1 GLASS OF DRY WHITE WINE

6 CUPS FISH STOCK (PAGE 37)

2-3 TABLESPOONS CHOPPED FRESH DILL

SERVES *6*

PREPARATION *20 minutes*

COOKING *about 1½ hours*

Calories per serving *513*
Total fat *Low*
Saturated fat *Low*
Protein *High*
Carbohydrate *Medium*
Cholesterol *300 mg*
Vitamins *B group, E*
Minerals *Potassium, Iron, Zinc, Selenium, Iodine*

1 First prepare the squid by pulling heads away from bodies. Slice the bodies open and empty them of all the innards. Dislodge and set aside the small elongated silver ink sacs. Slice off and discard the upper part of each head, keeping the tentacles with a thin collar-like stripe on top. Rinse thoroughly and drain. Slice everything in long thin strips.

2 Heat the oil in a medium saucepan and sauté the onions until they start to turn light golden. Add the prepared squid strips, turn up the heat, and sauté for about 10 minutes, turning continuously, until all the liquid evaporates and the squid starts to stick.

3 Add the wine with an equal quantity of water and season. Cover and cook gently for 15-20 minutes, until the squid is tender. Add the ink sacs and cook for 5 more minutes.

4 For the risotto you need a large wide-based saucepan or sauté pan. Fry the shallots and scallions in the olive oil until they glisten. Add the rice gradually and stir over gentle heat until it is coated in oil. Add the wine and, when it is all absorbed, start adding the hot fish stock gradually, a ladleful at a time, stirring constantly until it is absorbed.

5 After half an hour, add the squid and more seasoning and mix well. Continue adding the fish stock. About 5 minutes later, start tasting grains of rice. You may not need all the stock; the rice must be caught at the precise moment when it is tender but its middle still feels a little hard. It must not be overcooked, or it will become like a sticky ball.

6 Remove the pan from the heat, mix in the fresh dill, and serve immediately.

BURANI
A Princely Pilaf

Burani *was originally a family of eggplant dishes cooked for Princess Buran's wedding to the powerful Caliph al-Mamoun, son of Harun al-Rashid, in ninth-century Baghdad. Her real name was Khadijah, but she was better known under the pet name of Buran, after a Persian princess of the seventh century. There are still dishes called* braniya *in both Algeria and Morocco, which center around eggplant and meat. How could this lead to our present-day* burani *or* borani *or, in fact, the Indian* biryani, *which are all glorified pilafs? Such are the mysteries of culinary evolution! I suspect that the dish was transformed with the addition of grain in Turkey. Haven't the Ottomans been great lovers of rice, and aren't Turkish pilafs monumental and referred to by all sorts of literature, throughout the ages?*

I was introduced to burani *as a child by our next-door neighbors in Athens, a family of refugees from Smyrna who had fled the catastrophic war of 1922. The name of the dish made no sense to me until some years ago, when I read this story in an article by Charles Perry in the* Journal of Gastronomy. *It was such a splendid story that I love recounting it. It is my husband who has adopted* burani *now, and he regularly makes it in the summer on the island, when we have mounds of sugary tomatoes.*

We serve it with plain yogurt and a plate of feta or fresh goat cheese and a large green salad.

1 LARGE ONION, PEELED AND FINELY CHOPPED

3 TABLESPOONS OLIVE OIL

1 LARGE RED BELL PEPPER, THINLY SLICED

4 GARLIC CLOVES, MINCED

3 POUNDS RIPE TOMATOES, PEELED AND CHOPPED

1 TABLESPOON TOMATO PASTE

1¾ CUPS WATER

LARGE PINCH OF GROUND ALLSPICE

1 SMALL CINNAMON STICK OR A PINCH OF CINNAMON

½ TEASPOON SUGAR

1¾ CUPS LONG-GRAIN RICE

4 TABLESPOONS FINELY CHOPPED PARSLEY

PARSLEY SPRIGS FOR GARNISH (OPTIONAL)

2 TABLESPOONS FINELY CHOPPED FRESH DILL

SALT AND FRESHLY GROUND BLACK PEPPER

SERVES *4-5*

PREPARATION *20 minutes*

COOKING *35-40 minutes*

Calories per serving *438*
Total fat *Low*
Saturated fat *Low*
Protein *Low*
Carbohydrate *High*
Cholesterol *None*
Vitamins *A, B₁, B₃, B₆,*
Folate, C, E
Minerals *Potassium, Iron,*
Zinc, Iodine

1 Sauté the onion in the hot oil until light golden. Add the red pepper and, 2 minutes later, the garlic. Sauté everything together for a minute, without allowing it to brown.

2 Add the rest of the ingredients, apart from rice and the herbs, and simmer for 10 minutes until the sauce is thicker.

3 Mix in the rice and parsley. Season to taste,

cover, and cook gently until the water has been absorbed, approximately 15-20 minutes. Test the rice after 15 minutes and, if needed, add a little hot water.

4 When the rice is just tender, mix in the dill and remove from the heat. The dish should be quite moist and the rice not overcooked. Garnish with more parsley if you wish.

Burani

POLENTA

A few years ago, one of the many reasons I would look forward to going to Venice was to have polenta, but now instant versions have brought it to our door. Polenta is made with maize or cornmeal flour. Once cooked, it may be eaten as it is or prepared as below. You only need small portions of the polenta and a lot of sauce. Serve it with the squid on page 75, or with a thick tomato sauce (see page 32).

SERVES 4-6

PREPARATION 10
minutes

COOKING
*10-15 minutes, plus
cooling*

Calories per serving 193
Total fat *Medium*
Saturated fat *High*
Protein *Low*
Carbohydrate *Low*
Cholesterol *14 mg*
Vitamins *B₃*
Minerals *Iron, Zinc*

1¼ CUPS INSTANT POLENTA

½ TEASPOON SALT

2 TABLESPOONS BUTTER

1 TABLESPOON OLIVE OIL

1 Bring 3¾ cups of water to the boil in a large heavy pan and add the salt. Turn the heat down a little and add the polenta in a thin but steady stream, stirring constantly. Once it has all been added and starts to bubble, simmer for 3-4 minutes, continuing to stir to prevent sticking.
2 Turn the heat off, mix in the butter, and empty into an oiled quiche dish or other heatproof dish. Let stand for a few hours.
3 Just before serving, preheat a hot broiler, oil the top of the polenta, and broil for a few minutes, until the top is crisp and light golden. Cut it into thin slices and serve. Alternatively, cut the polenta into thicker wedges, oil these, and broil for 2 minutes on each side.

SAFFRON RICE WITH ORANGE AND NUTS

SERVES 4

PREPARATION
20-30 minutes

COOKING
10-15 minutes

Calories per serving 346
Total fat *Medium*
Saturated fat *Low*
Protein *Low*
Carbohydrate *High*
Cholesterol *None*
Vitamins *B₁, B₂, B₃, B₆,
Folate, C, E*
Minerals *Potassium, Zinc,
Iron*

¾ CUP LONG-GRAIN RICE, RINSED

2 LARGE PINCHES OF SAFFRON THREADS, CRUSHED

1 ORANGE, PEELED AND CUT INTO THIN DISCS

2 TABLESPOONS PINE NUTS, LIGHTLY TOASTED

GRATED ZEST AND JUICE OF 1 UNCOATED ORANGE

**2 TABLESPOONS SHELLED PISTACHIO NUTS, LIGHTLY
TOASTED AND CHOPPED**

½ CUP DRIED APRICOTS, COARSELY CHOPPED

2 TABLESPOONS SULTANAS OR RAISINS, RINSED

3 TABLESPOONS FINELY CHOPPED FRESH MINT

SALT

FOR THE VINAIGRETTE:

2 TABLESPOONS SHERRY VINEGAR

3 TABLESPOONS HAZELNUT OIL

1 TEASPOON SUNFLOWER OIL

1 Bring a pan of lightly salted water to the boil, add the rice and saffron, cover, and cook until the rice is tender but still quite firm. Drain and place the rice in a bowl.
2 Make the vinaigrette: whisk the vinegar together with the juice from the orange.
Season with salt, add the oils, and whisk again. Then pour over the rice while it is still warm.
3 Add the remaining ingredients and toss together to mix everything properly. Adjust the seasoning with some more salt, if necessary. Serve at room temperature.

Polenta, with black squid

SAFFRON PENNE SALAD
WITH TIGER PRAWNS

Pasta salads can make delicious impromptu meals and can be improvised with available ingredients. There are two rules for successful pasta salads. First, make sure that the pasta is slightly undercooked, so that it will hold its shape and texture when dressed. The second rule is to dress it while it is still hot and before it dries up and becomes sticky. Of course, a delicious vinaigrette is the most important ingredient. In the spring and early summer, one can have pasta with seasonal vegetables such as shelled fava beans and peas or asparagus and liven it up with fresh herbs. Alternatively, you can add grilled or roasted vegetables such as eggplant, zucchini, and bell peppers. Add some finely chopped fresh herbs and be bold with the vinaigrette. It could have a North African flavor if you season it with cumin, ginger, and garlic, or a tablespoon of harissa; you can use an olive or walnut oil with any of a number of vinegars, from Spanish sherry to Italian balsamic or a good French wine vinegar. It could even be a mixture of fresh farmer cheese or yogurt with olive oil and garlic…experiment!

If you are feeling extravagant you can add 4-6 scallops with the prawns (slice them in thin discs first), or some cooked and shelled mussels at the end.

SERVES *6 as a first course, or 4 as a main course*

PREPARATION *10 minutes*

COOKING *10-15 minutes, depending on the pasta*

Calories per serving *304*
Total fat *Low*
Saturated fat *Low*
Protein *High*
Carbohydrate *Medium*
Cholesterol *126 mg*
Vitamins *B group*
Minerals *Potassium, Iron, Zinc, Selenium, Iodine*

2 LARGE PINCHES OF SAFFRON THREADS, CRUMBLED

10 OUNCES PENNE

2 TABLESPOONS OLIVE OIL

8 OUNCES SHELLED COOKED TIGER PRAWNS OR OTHER JUMBO SHRIMP

2 GARLIC CLOVES, PEELED AND THINLY SLICED

5 OUNCES BUTTON MUSHROOMS

2 TABLESPOONS FINELY CHOPPED CHIVES

2-3 SPRIGS OF FRESH BASIL, TORN BY HAND

FOR THE VINAIGRETTE:

1½ TABLESPOONS BALSAMIC VINEGAR

1 GARLIC CLOVE, PEELED AND CRUSHED

2 TABLESPOONS OLIVE OIL

SALT AND FRESHLY GROUND BLACK PEPPER

1 Bring plenty of lightly salted water to the boil in a large pan, add the saffron, and then the pasta. Cook until the pasta is just al dente. Drain the pasta and turn it into a large bowl.
2 In the meantime, in a heavy-based or non-stick frying pan, heat the oil and add the prawns or shrimp and the garlic. Sauté these for 2 minutes, turn the heat up, and add the mushrooms, tossing everything together and turning them over brisk heat for about 3 minutes. Season to taste, add the chives and the basil, and sauté for 1 more minute, until the herbs look just wilted. Add this to the pasta in the bowl and mix together.
3 Whisk the vinegar, seasoning, and garlic for the vinaigrette together, then add the oil and whisk until well amalgamated. Adjust the seasoning. It should be quite sharp.
4 Add the vinaigrette to the pasta and toss gently to coat. It can now wait, covered with plastic wrap, if necessary. It can be served warm or slightly chilled in summer.

BULGARI PILAFI
Cracked Wheat and Vermicelli Pilaf

This earthy dish from the island of Cyprus is quick and easy to prepare, and makes a delicious partner to grilled poultry and meat, or casseroles of meat or vegetables. It goes well with plain yogurt or a yogurt sauce such as Sarimsakli Yogurt (page 33). It is the ideal standby dish, as the basic ingredients can happily live in the pantry for a long time.

3 TABLESPOONS OLIVE OIL
1 ONION, THINLY SLICED
¼ CUP VERMICELLI
2¼ CUPS COARSE

BULGAR, PICKED CLEAN
1½ CUPS CHICKEN STOCK (SEE PAGE **37**)
SALT AND FRESHLY GROUND BLACK PEPPER

1 Heat the oil gently in a saucepan and sauté the onion in it, stirring until the onion becomes translucent. Break up the vermicelli with your fingers and add it to the onion. Continue to stir until the vermicelli becomes pale golden and aromatic, about 2-3 minutes.
2 Rinse the bulgar in a fine sieve under running water and add it to the pan. Stir to mix it in and add the chicken stock and seasoning. Cover the pan and simmer gently for about 7-8 minutes, until the mixture looks almost dry.
3 Cover with a cloth, replace the lid on top, and let it stand off the heat for at least 10-15 minutes. It can wait like this for about 1 hour. When you uncover it you will be surprised by its lovely aroma. Any leftovers can be successfully reheated the next day, with a little added water.

SERVES *4*

PREPARATION
10 minutes

COOKING
about 30 minutes

Calories per serving *350*
Total fat *Low*
Saturated fat *Low*
Protein *Low*
Carbohydrate *High*
Cholesterol *None*
Vitamins B_1, B_3
Minerals *Potassium, Iron*

COUSCOUS SALAD WITH PEACHES, ARUGULA, AND PINE NUTS

This salad full of sunny flavors is an improvisation of mine. Other fruit, such as melon, pears, or strawberries, can be used instead of peaches. Served with soft cheeses—such as fresh goat cheese, ricotta or feta—and some fresh bread, it makes a lovely summer lunch particularly suited to a hot day. It also goes beautifully with marinated and grilled haloumi cheese (see page 53).

¾ CUP PRE-COOKED COUSCOUS (MOST COUSCOUS NOWADAYS IS PRE-COOKED)

½ CUP SKINNED ALMOND FLAKES

½ CUP PINE NUTS

8 OUNCES (2 OR 3) FIRM PEACHES, PEELED, PITTED, AND DICED SMALL

HANDFUL OF ARUGULA LEAVES, TRIMMED AND CHOPPED COARSELY IF THEY ARE LARGE

SMALL HANDFUL OF FRESH MINT, CHOPPED (RESERVING 1 OR 2 SPRIGS FOR GARNISH)

FOR THE VINAIGRETTE:

3 TABLESPOONS HAZELNUT OR ALMOND OIL

1 TEASPOON SUNFLOWER OIL

3 TABLESPOONS BALSAMIC VINEGAR

SALT

SERVES *4*

PREPARATION *30 minutes plus 1 hours' draining and 30 minutes' chilling*

Calories per serving *332*
Total fat *High*
Saturated fat *Low*
Protein *Low*
Carbohydrate *Low*
Cholesterol *None*
Vitamins *B₁, B₂, B₃, C, E*
Minerals *Iron, Zinc*

1 Soak the couscous in warm water to cover generously for 15 minutes. Drain for about an hour to dry completely, or roll it in a clean cloth to absorb excess moisture.

2 Place the almond flakes in a dry frying pan over gentle heat and keep shaking the pan for 1-2 minutes, until the nuts are lightly browned all over. Do the same with the pine nuts. Set the toasted nuts aside.

3 Mix the vinaigrette ingredients well, preferably briefly in a blender. Taste and adjust by perhaps adding a little more vinegar.

(Couscous makes a rather submissive partner, so it needs livening up.)

4 Half an hour before serving, place everything but the toasted nuts in a large bowl and toss gently to coat in the vinaigrette. In the summer the salad is more refreshing served lightly chilled, so cover with plastic wrap and place in the refrigerator at this stage.

5 To serve, mix in the toasted nuts, empty on a decorative platter (ideally a dark one to show off the colors) and decorate with the sprigs of mint.

Couscous Salad with Peaches, Arugula, and Pine Nuts

Fish & Shellfish

PROVENÇAL SEAFOOD STEW

There is nothing more glorious than an exotic mélange of seafood on a plate, surrounded by a smooth aromatic sauce. Freshness is the most important factor; otherwise the result of even the most expensive ingredients is poor or simply uninteresting.

SERVES *4-6*

PREPARATION *20 minutes*

COOKING *about 1 hour*

Calories per serving *492*
Total fat *Low*
Saturated fat *Low*
Protein *High*
Carbohydrate *Low*
Cholesterol *249 mg*
Vitamins *A, B group, E*
Minerals *Calcium, Potassium, Iron, Zinc, Selenium, Iodine*

2 TABLESPOONS OLIVE OIL

3-4 SHALLOTS, PEELED AND CHOPPED

1 SMALL LEEK, CHOPPED

1 TABLESPOON FENNEL SEEDS

2 GARLIC CLOVES, MINCED

12 OUNCES RIPE TOMATOES, SKINNED AND CHOPPED

2 LARGE PINCHES OF SAFFRON THREADS, CRUMBLED

1 GLASS OF WHITE WINE

GRATED ZEST AND JUICE OF 1 UNCOATED ORANGE

2 TABLESPOONS FRESH DILL, PLUS MORE TO GARNISH

5 CUPS GOOD FISH STOCK

SALT AND FRESHLY GROUND BLACK PEPPER

1-2 MEDIUM SQUID, PREPARED AS ON PAGE 75 BUT CUT INTO THIN RINGS

2 FILLETS OF JOHN DORY, RED BREAM, SEA BASS, HAKE OR COD, ABOUT 1 POUND IN TOTAL

2 FILLETS OF MONKFISH, ABOUT 1 POUND IN TOTAL

12 CLAMS, RINSED SEVERAL TIMES UNTIL CLEAN (OPTIONAL)

6-9 LANGOUSTINES OR RAW JUMBO SHRIMP IN THEIR SHELLS

2-3 SPRIGS OF FRESH OREGANO, CHOPPED

1 ZUCCHINI

1 CARROT

TO SERVE:

8 THIN SLICES OF FRENCH BAGUETTE, GRILLED UNTIL CRISP AND RUBBED WITH

2 GARLIC CLOVES

ROUILLE (PAGE 34)

1 Heat the oil gently in a large saucepan, add the shallots, leek, and fennel seeds, and sauté until the onion becomes translucent, about 5-7 minutes. Add the garlic, and a minute later the tomatoes and saffron. Turn with a spatula until the tomatoes look wilted.

2 Add the wine, orange zest and juice, dill, and stock. Season, cover, and boil steadily for 20-30 minutes.

3 Purée the mixture in a food processor. Then press it through a fine sieve to extract all the juices. Pour the sieved mixture back into the pan, taste and adjust the seasoning.

4 Bring this back to a boil, add the squid rings and tentacles, and cook gently for 15 minutes. Meanwhile, cut the fish into large cubes and add to the pan with the clams (if you are using them), langoustines or shrimp and oregano. Cook for 5 minutes more.

5 In the meantime, slice the zucchini and the carrot into long, thin, spaghetti-like strips and blanch them for 1 minute in lightly salted boiling water. Drain and refresh in cold water.

6 Place a selection of seafood in each warmed soup plate and pour the sauce over it. Top with some snipped dill. Serve with the strips of zucchini and carrot and the baguette croûtes spread with rouille.

Provençal Seafood Stew

PSAROSOUPA
Aegean Fish Soup

A few years ago when I was traveling around the Greek islands with illustrator Linda Smith, collecting material for our book Greek Island Cookery, *we inevitably sampled a fish soup on every island. They were all wonderful, but each one was different. The soup in Crete was made with* hristopsaro—*John Dory. In Rhodes, at the renowned Alexi's restaurant, the soup was made with grey mullet and tomatoes. On my home island of Alonnisos it is almost always made with the ferocious-looking bright-pink* skorpines—*scorpion fish—and never with tomatoes. In Mykonos it was made with the big-headed brown* rofos—*grouper—and so on. Basically they are all improvisations based on availability.*

When you are strolling round the waterfront in any of the Greek islands you will be dazzled by the fish on display at the restaurants. For a fish soup, all you have to do is choose your fish, have it weighed, and then come back in half an hour and your meal is ready—because a Greek island fish soup makes a complete meal. The fish is cooked with vegetables—most often potatoes, carrots, zucchini, and celery. The soup is then served separately and the fish is surrounded by the vegetables brought on a platter.

*In my opinion, the best soup is made with scorpion fish—*rascasse rouge *in French, and the main ingredient of the Provençal* bouillabaisse—*as its bones have a glutinous quality indispensable to a soup. Its huge head also adds a lot to the broth. A good alternative to this is red gurnard, which has a sweet taste. Dogfish is good, as is gray mullet; or a combination of different fish.*

These firm-fleshed fish need to cook for 20 minutes or more, for you to get the full benefit of the flavors in the broth. Scorpion fish needs at least half an hour's steady boiling. You can also strengthen the flavor by replacing some of the water with a broth made by boiling extra heads and bones of non-oily fish.

SERVES 6

PREPARATION 30 minutes

COOKING 45-50 minutes

Calories per serving 386
Total fat *Low*
Saturated fat *Low*
Protein *High*
Carbohydrate *Low*
Cholesterol 134 mg
Vitamins *A, B group*
Minerals *Calcium, Potassium, Iron, Zinc, Selenium, Iodine*

4 POUNDS MIXED FISH (SEE ABOVE), PREPARED WHOLE, RINSED AND DRAINED

2 TABLESPOONS OLIVE OIL, PLUS MORE TO SERVE

6-8 SMALL POTATOES, PEELED WHOLE

4-6 SMALL ONIONS, PEELED WHOLE

2 CARROTS, PEELED AND QUARTERED

1-2 SMALL STALKS OF CELERY, INCLUDING SOME LEAVES, CHOPPED

8 OUNCES ZUCCHINI, QUARTERED INTO 2-INCH LENGTHS

2 LEMONS

SALT AND FRESHLY GROUND BLACK PEPPER

1 Place the olive oil in a very large saucepan with 6 cups of water, bring to a boil and boil rapidly for 4-5 minutes in order to emulsify the liquid.

2 Season with salt and pepper and add the fish. Bring back to a boil and skim until clear.

Cover and cook for about 10 minutes.

3 Then add all the vegetables. They should be half-immersed in the broth, so add a little hot water if necessary, but beware of too much liquid as it will result in a tasteless soup. Cook for 20-30 minutes for large fish or less for

smaller ones, making sure the fish does not disintegrate. It must hold together so that it can be taken out whole, if possible. If the fish are small and cook more quickly, they should be taken out earlier and kept warm. Add in the juice of 1 lemon at the end.

4 Carefully take the fish out of the liquid, transfer it to a warmed platter, and surround it with the vegetables. Serve the soup separately and ask people to help themselves to a piece of fish and a selection of vegetables; or, if they prefer, they can have the soup first and the fish and vegetables afterward. Offer some olive oil and lemon wedges for the fish.

TURBOT WITH GINGER AND SAFFRON

This sumptuous dish is nevertheless extremely simple to prepare. Other types of fish—such as steaks of halibut, hake, brill, or monkfish—can be treated in the same manner, and they are all quite captivating. Serve the fish with piles of bright green mange-tout peas and broccoli florets, or the Fennel Gratin with Oil and Cheese on page 114.

4 TURBOT STEAKS, ABOUT 1¾ POUNDS IN TOTAL

2 TABLESPOONS OLIVE OIL

1 TABLESPOON BUTTER

1 INCH PIECE OF FRESH GINGERROOT, PEELED AND GRATED

⅔ CUP FISH STOCK, OR 1 GLASS OF DRY WHITE WINE

SALT AND FRESHLY GROUND BLACK PEPPER

2 LARGE PINCHES OF SAFFRON

3 TABLESPOONS LIGHT CREAM

2 TABLESPOONS FINELY CHOPPED FRESH CILANTRO, PLUS SOME WHOLE SPRIGS FOR GARNISH

SERVES *4*

PREPARATION *10-15 minutes*

COOKING *10-15 minutes*

Calories per serving *323*
Total fat *High*
Saturated fat *High*
Protein *High*
Carbohydrate *Low*
Cholesterol *15 mg*
Vitamins *B₂, B₁₂, B₃, B₁*
Minerals *Calcium, Potassium, Iron*

1 Wipe the fish clean. Heat the oil and butter gently in a large frying pan, add the ginger, and sauté for a few seconds, turning with a wooden spatula.

2 Add the turbot steaks to the pan and turn them over a couple of times to coat them in the oil and ginger. Continue to sauté the fish in this manner for 3-4 minutes.

3 Add the stock or wine and some seasoning. Bring to a gentle boil and add the saffron, crushing it with your fingers. Simmer for 5-6 minutes (or barely 4 minutes for hake), basting the fish a few times.

4 Take the fish out and transfer to a warm serving platter. If there is excess liquid in the pan, boil it rapidly to reduce it. Add the cream and the cilantro and simmer gently and briefly (about 2 minutes), stirring and scraping the residue in the pan until the sauce has thickened lightly.

5 Pour the sauce over the fish, decorate with the reserved cilantro sprigs, and serve.

BAKED RED MULLET WITH ORANGE

Red mullet is undoubtedly the king of the Mediterranean. Although the Mediterranean types are smaller and more bony than others, they are also more tasty. Other fish can be cooked in this way, such as red snapper, sea bream, or even filets of halibut, cod, or haddock.

SERVES 4

PREPARATION 10 minutes, plus 2 hours' marinating

COOKING 30 minutes

Calories per serving 380
Total fat *Medium*
Saturated fat *Low*
Protein *High*
Carbohydrate *Low*
Cholesterol *None*
Vitamins *B group, C, E*
Minerals *Calcium, Potassium, Iron, Zinc, Selenium, Iodine*

FEW SPRIGS OF FRESH DILL

4 WHOLE RED MULLETS OR 8 IF THEY ARE SMALL (ABOUT 2-3 POUNDS TOTAL WEIGHT), CLEANED

3 LARGE JUICY ORANGES

½ LEMON OR LIME

2 TABLESPOONS OLIVE OIL

SALT

2 TABLESPOONS TOASTED PINE NUTS

1 Two hours before cooking, place some fresh dill in the cavity of each fish and lay them side by side diagonally in a shallow oval oven dish, preferably glazed.

2 Squeeze the juice of 2 oranges and the lemon or lime. Mix these juices with the oil and pour over the fish. Leave to marinate for about 2 hours, spooning the marinade over the fish occasionally.

3 Preheat the oven to 350°F. Just before cooking, sprinkle a little salt all over the fish. Cut half of the remaining orange into thin slices, quarter these, and place a few quarters over each fish. Bake for 20 minutes.

4 Take out of the oven, baste, sprinkle with pine nuts, and return to the oven for 10 minutes.

5 Serve garnished with dill and the remaining orange half cut into quarter slices.

BAKED PRAWNS WITH TOMATOES

SERVES 4

PREPARATION 20 minutes

COOKING about 45 minutes

Calories per serving 250
Total fat *Medium*
Saturated fat *Medium*
Protein *High*
Carbohydrate *Low*
Cholesterol *209 mg*
Vitamins *A, B group, C, E*
Minerals *Calcium, Iron, Zinc, Selenium, Iodine*

2 TABLESPOONS OLIVE OIL

1 MEDIUM ONION, THINLY SLICED

1 GLASS OF DRY WHITE WINE

1½ POUNDS RIPE TOMATOES, BLANCHED, SKINNED AND CHOPPED

1 TEASPOON DRIED OREGANO

SALT AND FRESHLY GROUND BLACK PEPPER

14 OUNCES PEELED TIGER OR KING PRAWNS OR OTHER JUMBO SHRIMP

2 TABLESPOONS FINELY CHOPPED FRESH PARSLEY

4 OUNCES FETA OR MOZZARELLA CHEESE, CUBED

1 Preheat the oven to 350°F. Heat the oil in a frying pan and sauté the onion gently until translucent. Add the wine and boil for 3-4 minutes.

2 Add the tomatoes, oregano, and seasoning. Stir to mix everything and cook gently for

15-20 minutes, stirring occasionally, until the sauce looks quite thick.

3 Mix in the prawns or shrimp and parsley, empty the contents of the pan into an ovenproof dish, and sprinkle the cheese all over the top. Bake for 20 minutes. Serve hot.

Baked Red Mullet with Orange

SCALLOPS WITH MUSHROOMS

Scallops do not need a lot of cooking. Here, just searing quickly in a sparingly oiled frying pan is enough. An interesting variety of mushrooms alters the dish completely. The best is a mélange *of wild fungi.*

SERVES 4

PREPARATION 20 minutes

COOKING about 10 minutes

Calories per serving 185
Total fat *High*
Saturated fat *Low*
Protein *High*
Carbohydrate *Low*
Cholesterol 35 mg
Vitamins *A, B group, C, E*
Minerals *Potassium, Iron, Zinc, Selenium, Iodine*

10 SCALLOPS, SHELLED, RINSED AND DRAINED
2 GARLIC CLOVES, PEELED AND CRUSHED
8 OUNCES FIRM CHESTNUT OR OTHER MUSHROOMS
3 TABLESPOONS OLIVE OIL

1 RED BELL PEPPER, DESEEDED AND CUBED
2 TABLESPOONS FINELY CHOPPED PARSLEY
1 TABLESPOON FINELY CHOPPED CHERVIL
SALT AND FRESHLY GROUND BLACK PEPPER

1 Separate any roe from the scallops and set aside. Slice each scallop horizontally into two flat discs. Brush some olive oil over a ridged heavy cast-iron frying pan or a non-stick frying pan and on the scallops.
2 Place the remaining olive oil in another frying pan. When it is hot, add the sliced mushrooms and red pepper and stir over medium heat for 5-6 minutes.
3 Add some seasoning, the roe, the garlic, and the herbs, and cook for 2-3 minutes longer.
4 While the mushrooms and peppers are cooking, heat the pan for the scallops. When it is almost smoking, put in the scallops and cook them a minute on each side at most.
5 Toss into the mushroom mix and serve.

SQUID IN WINE SAUCE

SERVES 4 as a main course, or 6 as a first course

PREPARATION 20 minutes

COOKING about 1 hour

Calories per serving 452
Total fat *Medium*
Saturated fat *Low*
Protein *High*
Carbohydrate *Low*
Cholesterol 844 mg
Vitamins *B group, E*
Minerals *Potassium, Iron, Zinc, Selenium, Iodine*

3½ POUNDS MEDIUM-SIZED SQUID (ABOUT 3 OR 4)
12 OUNCES SLICED ONIONS
3 TABLESPOONS OLIVE OIL
2 STAR ANISE (OPTIONAL)

2 GLASSES OF DRY WHITE WINE
⅔ CUP HOT WATER
SALT AND FRESHLY GROUND BLACK PEPPER
3 TABLESPOONS CHOPPED PARSLEY OR CHERVIL

1 First clean the squid: pull first the head, and then the fins away from the body. Open the bodies up and discard all the innards. Pull off the outer skin and discard. Slice each head across and keep the tentacles, discarding the rest of the head. Rinse everything carefully, removing all traces of sand. Slice each body in half lengthwise and then cut into strips about 1 inch wide.
2 Sauté the onions in the olive oil in a saucepan over moderate heat. When the onions start to color, add the squid and star anise if you are using it. Sauté, stirring constantly, until all the water produced has evaporated and the squid starts to color. This will take about 15 minutes in all.
3 Slowly add the wine and, when the steam subsides, add the water and seasoning. Cover and cook slowly for about 20-30 minutes, until tender (depending on the size of the squid). It may start to stick, so stir occasionally and add a little more water as needed. You should be left with a delicious sweet thick sauce.
4 Add the herbs and cook for 2 minutes.

MEJILLONES A LA MARINERA
Mussels with Garlic and Wine

Mussels prepared quickly, as here, are served all over the Mediterranean, although they are most associated with France and Spain. Any good tapas *bar will display mussels among its intriguing array of appetizers. This recipe is almost identical to French* moules marinières, *but for the addition of saffron. In countries such as Greece and Turkey there are a whole range of dishes with mussels. Once they have been prepared and cooked quickly, almost in the same way as here, they are then shelled and made into delicious pilafs or dipped into garlicky breadcrumbs and fried or grilled. In Turkey, large mussels are stuffed with a delicious filling made of rice, tiny currants, and pine nuts.*

3½ POUNDS MUSSELS

2 TABLESPOONS OLIVE OIL

3-4 SHALLOTS OR 1 MEDIUM ONION, THINLY SLICED

2 GARLIC CLOVES, PEELED AND CRUSHED

2-3 SPRIGS OF FRESH THYME, CHOPPED

2-3 SMALL TOMATOES, SKINNED AND DICED

(OPTIONAL)

⅔ CUP WHITE WINE

FRESHLY GROUND PEPPER

LARGE PINCH OF SAFFRON THREADS, CRUMBLED

2 TABLESPOONS FINELY CHOPPED CHERVIL OR PARSLEY, TO GARNISH

SERVES *4*

PREPARATION *about 30 minutes*

COOKING
10-15 minutes, plus 5 minutes' standing

Calories per serving *333*
Total fat *Medium*
Saturated fat *Low*
Protein *High*
Carbohydrate *Low*
Cholesterol *133 mg*
Vitamins *B group, E*
Minerals *Calcium, Potassium, Iron, Zinc, Selenium, Iodine*

1 Wash the mussels under running water, scraping them with a knife to remove barnacles and beards. Place them in a sink or bowl filled with water for 10 minutes, letting their grit sink, and lift them out by hand. Repeat this process several times until the water is clear. At the same time, get rid of any mussels with broken shells or any that remain open when tapped.

2 Heat the oil in a large saucepan, add the shallots or onion, and sauté until glistening. Add the garlic and thyme. Sauté together until the mixture is aromatic, then add the tomatoes if you are using them (they do add sweetness) and stir for 2 minutes.

3 Pour in the wine. Add some pepper and the saffron. Let the mixture bubble for 2-3 minutes, then add the mussels. Turn the heat up, cover, and cook briskly for 4-5 minutes, shaking the pan vigorously a few times, until the mussels have opened. Take the mussels out with a slotted spoon and place them in a large warmed bowl. Discard any mussels that remain closed.

4 Let the cooking liquid stand for 5 minutes to let any grit sink to the bottom. Ideally the liquid should be strained through cheesecloth over the mussels at this stage. Otherwise, tilt the pan carefully and pour the liquid out, leaving behind any gritty traces. Sprinkle the herbs over the top and serve immediately in soup bowls, offering plenty of crusty bread.

HAKE IN RED PEPPER COULIS

Mediterranean hake has a subtle, clean taste that is often used as a background to playful flavors and textures. It is commonly served baked with pepper and tomato sauce. In Spain it becomes merluza en salsa verde, *and in this recipe it is combined with a Provençal explosion of color and tastes in a red pepper coulis. Filets of John Dory or sea bass can also be served in the same way. This dish goes well with the Catalan Spinach on page 117.*

SERVES *4*

PREPARATION *about 30 minutes*

COOKING *about 10 minutes*

Calories per serving *282*
Total fat *Medium*
Saturated fat *Low*
Protein *High*
Carbohydrate *Low*
Cholesterol *40 mg*
Vitamins *A, Folate, B6, C, E*
Minerals *Iron, Potassium*

2 TABLESPOONS OLIVE OIL
2 GARLIC CLOVES, PEELED AND CRUSHED
4 HAKE FILLETS, EACH WEIGHING ABOUT 6 OUNCES, OR 8 SMALLER FILLETS, ABOUT 3-4 OUNCES
1 SMALL GLASS OF WHITE WINE
HANDFUL OF BASIL LEAVES
SALT AND FRESHLY GROUND BLACK PEPPER

LEMON SLICES, TO GARNISH

FOR THE RED PEPPER COULIS:
3 MEDIUM-SIZED RED BELL PEPPERS
1 TEASPOON OLIVE OIL
1½ TABLESPOONS BALSAMIC VINEGAR

1 First make the coulis: preheat a moderate broiler. Place the peppers in the broiler pan, arrange them about 2 inches from the heat and broil for about 10 minutes, turning 2-3 times until charred evenly all over.

2 When the peppers are cool enough to handle, peel or scrape off their charred skins as neatly as possible and discard. Trim and discard the tops, seeds and thick inner membranes.

3 Place the pepper flesh and juices in a food processor with a little hot water, and process to a smooth paste. Put this through a fine sieve, pressing and scraping to get all the juices through. Add the oil and vinegar, and mix them in. Cover the coulis and set aside.

4 Now cook the fish: heat the oil gently in a large sauté pan, add the garlic, and stir briefly. Then add the fillets, skin side down, and sauté gently for 2 minutes without allowing them to brown. Immediately add the wine, most of the basil torn by hand, and salt and pepper. Tilt the pan to coat the fish and cook gently for 3-4 more minutes, basting the fish occasionally. Hake really needs very little cooking.

5 Lift the fillets from the pan and transfer to individual warmed plates. Reduce the juices in the pan by boiling rapidly for a couple of minutes, pour them over the filets. Surround each fillet with the coulis and garnish with the remaining basil leaves and some lemon slices.

Hake in Red Pepper Coulis

NORTH AFRICAN MONKFISH

Monkfish, with its layer of tastes and its wonderful texture, always produces astounding dishes. However, this must be the best and the easiest of them all, and has been a favorite of anyone who has tried it.

SERVES 4

PREPARATION 20 minutes

COOKING about 15 minutes

Calories per serving 148
Total fat High
Saturated fat Low
Protein High
Carbohydrate Low
Cholesterol 14 mg
Vitamins B₃
Minerals Iron, Iodine

2 MONKFISH TAILS, SKINNED, MEMBRANE REMOVED, BONED AND CUT INTO 4 LONG FILLETS (ABOUT 3 POUNDS ON THE BONE)
3 TABLESPOONS OLIVE OIL
2-3 GARLIC CLOVES, PEELED AND CRUSHED

1-INCH PIECE OF FRESH GINGER ROOT, PEELED AND GRATED
1 TABLESPOON GROUND CUMIN
LARGE HANDFUL OF CILANTRO, FINELY CHOPPED
SALT AND FRESHLY GROUND BLACK PEPPER

1 Rinse and dry the fish. It is important to dry it properly; otherwise it will produce a lot of moisture while cooking, and it should not be swimming in a bath of water. Cut each fillet into 3-4 large cubes, about double bite-sized.
2 Heat the oil gently in a large frying pan. Add the garlic, sauté briefly until aromatic, and immediately add the ginger. After a few seconds, add the cumin while stirring continuously. The mixture should not burn, but the cumin oils will become aromatic.
3 Turn the heat up in order to seal the fish.

Add the fish and keep stirring to coat it all in this mixture. Let it cook for about 6-8 minutes (monkfish is quite a muscular fish), stirring gently from time to time. Once the fish is sealed turn the heat down. When the fish is cooked to your liking (take a piece out and try it, as it should not be hard at this stage), add salt, pepper, and the cilantro, and stir quickly for 2 or 3 minutes more. It should be quite dry by then, but with a delicious sauce.
4 Serve with spinach or leeks and small boiled potatoes, or with a large colorful salad.

SWORDFISH BROCHETTES

There is excitement whenever a kaiki *with a huge swordfish on board comes into the small harbor of Patitiri on the Aegean island of Alonnisos. Sometimes two or three children will be seen carrying the glistening creature to a particular restaurant. Apart from pleasing the eye, it also means feasting the palate, as* xifias souvlaki, *or swordfish brochettes, will be featured in most restaurants. If the* souvlakia *are to be served al fresco, a large salad and lots of fresh bread will be accompaniment enough; otherwise serve the skewers with steamed broccoli and boiled potatoes.*

SERVES 4

PREPARATION 15 minutes, plus 4-5 hours' marinating

COOKING 4-8 minutes

2 POUNDS SWORDFISH
2 TABLESPOONS OLIVE OIL
JUICE OF 1½ LEMONS
SMALL BUNCH OF FRESH MARJORAM, FINELY

CHOPPED, OR 1 TABLESPOON DRIED OREGANO
SALT AND FRESHLY GROUND BLACK PEPPER
2 GREEN BELL PEPPERS
1 RED ONION, PEELED AND QUARTERED

1 Slice the fish into large bite-sized cubes. Beat the oil, lemon juice, herbs, and seasoning together and toss the fish in this until it is well coated. Cover and leave to marinate for 3-4 hours in the refrigerator.

2 Slice the peppers into quarters, trim, and discard the seeds and stalks. If the quarters are too large, slice each one across the middle. Take the onion layers apart.

3 About 30 minutes before the fish is to be cooked, thread the cubes on 4-6 metal skewers, alternating with pieces of onion and pepper. Brush the skewers with the marinade.

4 Grill the souvlakia briefly on charcoal for about 3-4 minutes on each side, or simply broil (not too near the heat) for 2-3 minutes only on each side. Once they have been turned over, brush again with the marinade to keep them moist.

Calories per serving *309*
Total fat *Low*
Saturated fat *Low*
Protein *High*
Carbohydrate *Low*
Cholesterol *99 mg*
Vitamins *B group, E*
Minerals *Potassium, Iron, Iodine*

SPICY GRILLED TUNA WITH ARUGULA

There is something spectacular about a fresh tuna steak cooking over a charcoal fire by the sea in September. Tuna, with its rich flavors, responds well to marinades, and should be accompanied by something that provides a sharp contrast. If arugula is unavailable, use watercress instead.

4 THIN TUNA STEAKS, EACH ABOUT 5 OUNCES
BUNCH OF ARUGULA OR 4 OUNCES ARUGULA LEAVES
1 TABLESPOON OLIVE OIL

FOR THE MARINADE:
1 TABLESPOON OLIVE OIL
JUICE OF 1-2 LARGE LEMONS
2 GARLIC CLOVES, PEELED AND CRUSHED
¾-INCH PIECE OF FRESH GINGERROOT, GRATED
½ TEASPOON GROUND CUMIN
HANDFUL OF FRESH CILANTRO, FINELY CHOPPED
SALT AND FRESHLY GROUND BLACK PEPPER

SERVES *4*

PREPARATION *15 minutes, plus 3-4 hours' marinating*

COOKING *4-8 minutes*

1 Lay the tuna in one layer on a platter. Beat the marinade ingredients together with some seasoning and pour it over the steaks. Cover and chill in the refrigerator for 3-4 hours, turning the steaks over a couple of times.

2 Grilling over charcoal in the open air always has the best results. Lift the steaks from the marinade and place them in a grill basket. This will prevent them from breaking up. Grill for about 3-4 minutes on each side, according to how hot your barbecue is. Alternatively, if you are using a conventional broiler, cook the steaks very quickly under a high heat, about 1-2 minutes on each side, so that they are still juicy in the middle. Tuna goes papery when overcooked.

3 While the tuna is cooking, boil the marinade in a small pan to reduce it a little.

4 At the last minute, heat the oil gently in a frying pan and toss the arugula in it rapidly. It should only turn bright green and wilt but not cook; this takes less than 1 minute.

5 Divide the arugula between 4 plates and place the steaks on top of it. Drizzle the marinade over the steaks and serve.

Calories per serving *263*
Total fat *High*
Saturated fat *Low*
Protein *High*
Carbohydrate *Low*
Cholesterol *39 mg*
Vitamins *B group*
Minerals *Potassium, Iron, Zinc, Selenium, Iodine*

Meat & Poultry

OSSOBUCO ALLA ROMANA
Roman Braised Shin of Veal

Ossobuchi *are medium-thick slices of a shin of veal that are braised slowly until they are meltingly sweet.* Ossobuco *always constitutes a treat, with its tantalizing taste and pampering texture. Originally a Milanese dish—the name actually means "bone with a hole," according to Marcella Hazan—it contains tomatoes and is traditionally served with* risotto alla Milanese, *a saffron and bone marrow risotto.*

A long time ago we had a very different version in a small lunch-time restaurant almost under the shade of the Vatican in Rome. To my mind this is the purest version I have ever had, and it is now the only way I cook it. Served with delicious spinach and sautéed potatoes, it is also much simpler and lighter. Here it is—a purist's dish.

SERVES *4*

PREPARATION
10 minutes

COOKING
about 1¾ hours

Calories per serving *367*
Total fat *Low*
Saturated fat *Low*
Protein *High*
Carbohydrate *Low*
Cholesterol *130 mg*
Vitamins *B group, E*
Minerals *Potassium, Iron, Zinc, Selenium, Iodine*

2 TABLESPOONS OLIVE OIL

4 PIECES OF VEAL SHANK, EACH ABOUT 1 INCH THICK
(TOTAL WEIGHT ABOUT 2¼ POUNDS)

2 TABLESPOONS FLOUR

5-6 FRESH SAGE LEAVES

⅔ CUP DRY WHITE WINE

1¾ CUPS HOT BEEF OR CHICKEN STOCK

A FEW LONG PIECES OF FRESH OR DRIED ORANGE PEEL
(FROM AN UNCOATED ORANGE)

SALT AND FRESHLY GROUND BLACK PEPPER

5-6 BASIL LEAVES, TORN BY HAND

1 Choose a large and heavy-based casserole or other pan with a tight-fitting lid in which the ossobuco will fit in a single layer, and heat the oil in it. Pat the meat dry and coat it lightly in flour. Shake off excess flour and, when the oil is quite hot, brown the meat quickly on both sides. It should be light golden in color.

2 Once the meat is ready add the sage leaves, and a minute later pour in the wine. Let it bubble and evaporate for a few minutes, then add the stock, the orange peel, and season to taste. Cover tightly and cook very gently for

about 1½ hours, until the meat is very soft. Turn the meat over carefully a couple of times during the cooking time, but be careful not to spill the marrow from its center.

3 Once the meat is ready, sprinkle the basil leaves over it, cover again, and simmer for a few more minutes. By now the sauce will be thick and velvety. Serve with Catalan Spinach (page 117) or steamed small zucchini and mashed potatoes made with olive oil instead of butter.

Ossobuco alla Romana

BULGAR KEBABI
Ground Lamb and Cracked Wheat Kebabs

SERVES 6

PREPARATION 20
minutes , plus 30
minutes' soaking

COOKING
about 12 minutes

Calories per serving 453
Total fat *High*
Saturated fat *Low*
Protein *High*
Carbohydrate *Low*
Cholesterol 46 mg
Vitamins *A, B group, E*
Minerals *Potassium, Iron, Zinc*

3 OUNCES FINE BULGAR (CRACKED WHEAT)
2¼ POUNDS LEAN GROUND LAMB
1 EGG
1 LARGE ONION, COARSELY GRATED
3 GARLIC CLOVES, CRUSHED
4 TABLESPOONS FINELY CHOPPED FRESH MINT
5 SPRIGS OF FLAT-LEAVED PARSLEY, FINELY CHOPPED
½ TEASPOON GROUND ALLSPICE
1½ TEASPOONS PAPRIKA

½ TEASPOON CAYENNE OR ANTEP PEPPER
1½ OUNCES PINE NUTS, COARSELY CHOPPED
SALT AND FRESHLY GROUND BLACK PEPPER

TO SERVE:
HOT FLAT PITA BREAD
THINLY SLICED ONION RINGS, SPRINKLED WITH URFA PEPPER (SEE PAGE 15)
GRILLED TOMATO SLICES
SMALL PLATE OF ANTEP PEPPER (SEE PAGE 15)

1 Rinse the bulgar briefly. Put in a bowl, cover with hot water, and leave to soak for 20 minutes. Drain and squeeze out excess water.
2 Mix the bulgar with the lamb and the egg, and then mix in the remaining ingredients. Season the mixture and work it with your hands until it is well amalgamated. Make it into 18 medium-sized elongated flat patties.

3 Grill the patties in 2 batches, for about 3 minutes on each side. Keep the first warm while the second batch is cooking.
4 While the kebabs are grilling, prepare a small platter with some onion rings sprinkled with urfa pepper. Serve with hot pita, grilled tomatoes, small plates of antep pepper for dipping the kebabs, and a large mixed salad.

ALBONDIGAS
Spanish Meatballs

Albondigas *are ubiquitous in Spain, as they are to be found on every bar among the* tapas.

MAKES 30-35 *small meatballs*

PREPARATION 20-25
minutes

COOKING
40 minutes

1½ POUNDS GROUND BEEF (OR LAMB AND BEEF)
1 MEDIUM ONION, COARSELY GRATED
3 GARLIC CLOVES, PEELED AND CRUSHED
1 EGG
2 TABLESPOONS GROUND ALMONDS
1 TABLESPOON PIMENTÓN DULCE (SEE PAGE 14) OR PAPRIKA
1 TABLESPOON GROUND CUMIN
¼ TEASPOON GROUND CINNAMON

4 TABLESPOONS FINELY CHOPPED PARSLEY

FOR THE SAUCE:
2 TABLESPOONS PEANUT OIL
2 TABLESPOONS FENNEL SEEDS
1 GLASS OF WHITE WINE
2 TABLESPOONS ANISE, PERNOD OR RICARD
14-OUNCE CAN OF CHOPPED TOMATOES
1 TABLESPOON TOMATO PASTE

1 Mix all the ingredients for the meatballs in a large bowl. Take small handfuls of the mixture and shape them into walnut-sized balls.
2 Next make the sauce: heat the oil gently in a large heavy pan with a lid, add the fennel seeds and swirl them around until they start to sizzle. Add the wine and the anise and simmer for 2 minutes. Add the tomatoes with their liquid, the tomato paste diluted in ⅔ cup of water, and season. Simmer gently for 10 minutes.
3 Add the meatballs and roll to coat in the sauce. Cover and simmer for 20-30 minutes. Turn them over carefully once during that time and add a little water if needed.

Calories per meatball *52*
Total fat *High*
Saturated fat *High*
Protein *High*
Carbohydrate *Low*
Cholesterol *10 mg*
Vitamins B₃, B₆, B₁₂, E
Minerals *Iron, Zinc*

MOROCCAN GRILLED KOFTA

2 POUNDS GROUND LAMB (OR LAMB AND BEEF)
1 LARGE ONION, COARSELY GRATED
1-INCH PIECE OF FRESH GINGERROOT, PEELED AND GRATED
1 TABLESPOON GROUND CUMIN
1 TEASPOON GROUND CORIANDER SEEDS
½ TEASPOON ALLSPICE

½ TEASPOON RAS-EL-HANOUT (OPTIONAL, PAGE 23)
¼ TEASPOON CAYENNE PEPPER
1 TEASPOON PAPRIKA
1 EGG
4 TABLESPOONS FINELY CHOPPED PARSLEY
4 TABLESPOONS FINELY CHOPPED CILANTRO
SALT AND FRESHLY GROUND BLACK PEPPER

SERVES *4*

PREPARATION *25 minutes, plus 1-2 hours' resting*

COOKING *10-12 minutes*

Calories per serving *378*
Total fat *High*
Saturated fat *Low*
Protein *High*
Carbohydrate *Low*
Cholesterol *58 mg*
Vitamins A, B group
Minerals *Potassium, Iron, Zinc*

1 Ideally the ground meat should have been through the machine twice. Greek butchers do this automatically, and it results in a much better-blended kofta and a more pleasing, softer texture. Combine all the ingredients in a bowl, season, and mix vigorously with your hands in order to blend properly and achieve a silky texture. Cover and let rest for 1-2 hours in the refrigerator.
2 Shape the rested mixture into sausage shapes about 4 inches long and pass a flat metal skewer through the middle of each. Arrange 2-3 patties on each skewer. Squeeze the meat around the skewer in order to make it thinner and longer and squeeze the 2 edges in so that it stays firmly on the skewer. They should not be too heavy or they will fall off.
3 Grill the kebabs, either over charcoal or in the kitchen under a preheated broiler on a lightly oiled broiler pan for 10-12 minutes in all, turning them carefully around 2-3 times until they are crisp and golden all over.

CHICKEN WITH FORTY CLOVES OF GARLIC

I still remember the first time we had a dish similar to this, cooked with rabbit by Jill Norman, the cookery editor and publisher, who is also an imaginative and skillful cook. When the casserole was brought to the dinner table and its lid lifted, the aromas that engulfed us were sensational.

In Provence, lamb is also baked with this amount of garlic underneath it. The dish is in a class by itself when the garlic used is young and fresh, with plump juicy pink cloves. When the garlic is old it becomes almost acrid and rather bitter-tasting, particularly when roasted.

The chicken can be roasted whole or cut into pieces beforehand for the sake of convenience.

3 TABLESPOONS OLIVE OIL
1 CHICKEN, WEIGHING ABOUT 3¼ POUNDS, WHOLE OR CUT INTO 4-6 PIECES
40 GARLIC CLOVES, UNPEELED
2 CARROTS, SLICED
2 TABLESPOONS COARSELY CHOPPED TARRAGON
3-4 SPRIGS OF FRESH THYME, COARSELY CHOPPED
2 TABLESPOONS BRANDY
1 GLASS OF WHITE WINE, SUCH AS A WHITE CÔTES-DU-RHÔNE
SALT AND FRESHLY GROUND BLACK PEPPER

SERVES *4*

PREPARATION *10 minutes*

COOKING *about 1¾ hours*

Calories per serving *259*
Total fat *Low*
Saturated fat *Low*
Protein *High*
Carbohydrate *Low*
Cholesterol *171 mg*
Vitamins *B group*
Minerals *Potassium, Iron, Zinc, Sellenium, Iodine*

1 Preheat the oven to 325°F. Heat the oil gently in a large heavy-based ovenproof casserole. Place the chicken or chicken pieces in it and sauté for 8-10 minutes, turning until light golden all over. Remove the chicken and transfer to a plate.

2 Place the garlic, carrots, and herbs in the casserole and sauté them for 3-4 minutes, turning with a spatula.

3 Put the chicken back in the casserole and pour the brandy and the wine over it. Simmer for 3-4 minutes. Sprinkle in some seasoning, cover tightly, and cook in the oven for 1½ hours.

4 Take the casserole to the table and lift the lid there for the full aromatic effect. Serve the chicken with some of the garlic cloves, which will have become quite creamy inside and should be squeezed out of their shells either on the chicken or on bread. Lightly steamed crunchy French beans go perfectly with this dish, as well as plain boiled small potatoes for those with large appetites.

Chicken with Forty Cloves of Garlic

MAGRET OF DUCK WITH POMEGRANATES

The arrival of fall is signaled for me when the scarlet pomegranates look bulging on the trees in September. By October, in an area as beautiful as Pelion in Greece, the landscape is transformed. The leaves are turning shades of copper and starting to fall on the mossy ground. The brilliantly colored fruit then looks even more glorious on the trees. Pomegranates, quinces, and apples hanging on the boughs amid the autumnal riot of colors and mellow light attain a magical quality.

At this time of the year I love visiting my sister at her house in Tsangaratha in Pelion, and there we indulge ourselves in seasonal follies. Everything we cook has some of the fruit from the garden, and to crown it all in the evening we roast chestnuts on the fire. Utter seasonal bliss.

SERVES *4*

PREPARATION *25 minutes*

COOKING *45-50 minutes*

Calories per serving *359*
Total fat *High*
Saturated fat *Medium*
Protein *High*
Carbohydrate *Low*
Cholesterol *186 mg*
Vitamins *B group*
Minerals *Iron, Zinc, Potassium*

4 MAGRETS (DUCK BREASTS), TOTAL WEIGHT ABOUT 1½ POUNDS, OR 2 LARGE ONES

1½ TABLESPOONS AROMATIC HONEY

2 TABLESPOONS LEMON JUICE

PINCH OF GROUND CINNAMON

SALT AND FRESHLY GROUND BLACK PEPPER

FOR THE POMEGRANATE SAUCE:

2 SHALLOTS, SLICED

2 TABLESPOONS OLIVE OIL

1 GLASS OF AMONTILLADO OR FINO SHERRY

SEEDS FROM 2 POMEGRANATES, WITHOUT THE YELLOW PITH (SEE PAGE 19)

1 TABLESPOON BALSAMIC VINEGAR

1 Prepare the sauce in advance (the duck breasts must be cooked just before they are to be served). Sauté the shallots in the oil over gentle heat until translucent. Add the sherry, let it bubble for 2 minutes and then add the pomegranate seeds and any reserved juices. Simmer for 15 minutes and let it cool a little.

2 Purée the sauce in a blender or food processor and pass it through a fine sieve. Pour back into the pan and set aside.

3 Preheat the oven to 425°F. Trim excess fat from the magrets and wipe them with a paper towel. Using a small sharp knife, score the skins with a criss-cross pattern. Season and place them side by side on a rack, skin-side down over a roasting pan.

4 Half an hour before they are to be served, place the magrets in the oven and cook for 10 minutes. Take out and drain off all the fat.

5 Beat the honey, lemon juice and cinnamon together with some seasoning and paint this over the breasts generously. Turn the magrets over skin-side up and brush this side also. Cook for 15-20 minutes more, according to size and individual taste (but they should still be pink in the middle).

6 Just before serving, finish the sauce: add the juices from the duck, season, and simmer for 5 minutes. Finally add the vinegar.

7 Warm 4 plates. Cut each breast into slices and arrange them in the middle of each plate. Surround with the pomegranate sauce and serve with steamed fine French green beans and small boiled potatoes.

Magret of Duck with Pomegranates

MARINATED BROILED POUSSIN

The trick with this delicious and easy dish is to organize yourself well in advance, as the marinating accounts for all the tantalizing flavors. It is best if you can marinate overnight, or for at least 6 hours.

This makes an ideal summer dish, served with a large and colorful salad of different leaves such as Romaine, curly endive, radicchio, and some arugula and fennel with scallions. It also goes well with strips of roasted peppers dressed with a vinaigrette of olive oil and balsamic vinegar.

SERVES *4*

PREPARATION *30 minutes, plus overnight marinating*

COOKING *10-15 minutes*

Calories per serving *315*
Total fat *High*
Saturated fat *Medium*
Protein *High*
Carbohydrate *Low*
Cholesterol *149 mg*
Vitamins *B group*
Minerals *Iron, Zinc, Potassium, Selenium*

4 POUSSINS (VERY YOUNG, SMALL CHICKENS), CUT INTO TWO LENGTHWISE

FOR THE MARINADE:
3 TABLESPOONS OLIVE OIL
2 GARLIC CLOVES, CRUSHED
1-INCH PIECE OF FRESH GINGERROOT, PEELED AND FINELY GRATED
JUICE OF 1 LARGE LEMON
1 TEASPOON FRESH OR DRIED OREGANO OR THYME
SALT AND FRESHLY GROUND BLACK PEPPER

1 Lay the chicken halves skin-side up on a flat platter. Beat the marinade ingredients together lightly and, using a spoon, spread some over each piece. Leave to stand for about 30 minutes. Turn each piece over and repeat the process, making sure that most surfaces are coated. Cover with plastic wrap and place in the refrigerator overnight if possible.

2 Preheat the broiler, place the chicken pieces skin-side down on a broiler rack, and broil under low-to-medium heat for about 5-6 minutes or until they start to brown. Turn over, brush with some of the marinade juices and cook slowly for 6-8 minutes until the skin starts to blister. If you have to cook them in 2 batches, keep the first batch in a warm oven while cooking the remaining pieces.

3 Alternatively, make the meal informal and encourage people to start eating the chicken as it comes straight from the broiler.

LAMB AND ROMAINE CASSEROLE

One of the best dishes in Greek cooking, this is found on the islands and the mainland alike in the spring, around Easter. If one meat dish was to represent each Mediterranean country this should be the one for Greece. It is made with a leg of lamb, which is leaner than a shoulder; however, the latter can be used trimmed. Serve with fresh crusty bread.

SERVES *4-6*

PREPARATION *20 minutes*

COOKING *about 1½ hours*

2¼ POUNDS BONED LEG OF LAMB, CUBED LARGE
2 TABLESPOONS SUNFLOWER OIL
1 MEDIUM ONION, THINLY SLICED
4 CUPS HOT WATER
SALT
2 LARGE ROMAINE LETTUCES, SHREDDED
4-5 SCALLIONS, CHOPPED
4 TABLESPOONS COARSELY CHOPPED FRESH DILL
EGG-AND-LEMON SAUCE (PAGE 36)

1 Wipe the meat clean. Heat the oil in a large heavy-based pan and sauté the onions until glistening. Turn the heat up, add the meat and sauté, stirring, for about 10 minutes or until all the liquid evaporates.

2 Add the hot water and some salt, cover, and cook for 50-60 minutes, until the meat is tender but not falling apart. Mix in the lettuces, scallions, and dill, cover, and cook gently for 15 more minutes.

3 Let the dish stand for 5 minutes before adding the egg sauce. Beat the eggs lightly, add the cornstarch, and beat until smooth. Add the lemon juice and beat together briefly. Then gradually add 4-5 tablespoons of the hot liquid while beating continuously.

4 Pour the sauce over the meat and rotate the pan, until well incorporated. Return to a gentle heat for 1-2 minutes, just to warm the sauce through without allowing it to boil.

Calories per serving *423*
Total fat *High*
Saturated fat *Low*
Protein *High*
Carbohydrate *Low*
Cholesterol *99 mg*
Vitamins *A, B group, C, E*
Minerals *Potassium, Iron, Zinc, Iodine*

MOROCCAN CHICKEN TAJINE

2 TABLESPOONS OLIVE OIL
1 LARGE ONION, THINLY SLICED
5 GARLIC CLOVES, PEELED AND CRUSHED
1-INCH PIECE OF FRESH GINGERROOT, GRATED
2 PINCHES OF SAFFRON THREADS, CRUMBLED
1 TABLESPOON CARAWAY SEEDS
1½ TABLESPOONS GROUND CUMIN
1 TEASPOON PAPRIKA
¼ TEASPOON CAYENNE PEPPER
1 CHICKEN, WEIGHING ABOUT 3¼ POUNDS, CUT INTO 6-8 PIECES
⅔ CUP HOT WATER
1 PRESERVED LEMON (PAGE 19), FINELY CHOPPED

LARGE HANDFUL OF CILANTRO, COARSELY CHOPPED
2 CUPS BLACK OLIVES, RINSED
SALT AND FRESHLY GROUND BLACK PEPPER

FOR THE COUSCOUS:
2½ CUPS PRE-COOKED COUSCOUS
1 TABLESPOON OLIVE OIL
1¼ PINTS HOT CHICKEN BROTH OR WATER

SERVES *4*

PREPARATION *20 minutes*

COOKING *1¼-1¾ hours*

Calories per serving *519*
Total fat *Medium*
Saturated fat *Low*
Protein *High*
Carbohydrate *Low*
Cholesterol *105 mg*
Vitamins *B group, E*
Minerals *Iron, Potassium, Selenium*

1 Heat the oil in a large ovenproof saucepan and sauté the onion until translucent. Add the garlic, ginger, and spices, and sauté together briefly until aromatic. Add the chicken pieces and turn them around with a spatula for 2-3 minutes to coat them in the spices. Add the hot water and the preserved lemon with some seasoning. Cover and either simmer for 50 minutes or cook in the oven preheated to 325°F for 1 hour.

2 Add the cilantro and the olives to the pan and simmer for 10 more minutes, or return to the oven for 15 minutes more.

3 Half an hour before serving, prepare the couscous: spread it in a large attractive gratin dish, add the oil, some salt, and the broth or water. Mix and let it stand for 15 minutes. Fluff it a little with a fork and place in the oven with the chicken for 5 minutes just to warm it through before serving.

Vegetables
& Legumes

IMAM BAYILDI
Turkish-Style Baked Eggplant

Legend has it that the Turkish Imam fainted after indulging in this dish (bayildi means "fainted"). Was it because of overindulgence, or his shock at the amount of olive oil that his wife had used in the dish? We will never know. In this version, however, the amount of oil used would not have caused the Imam any distress, although the sumptuousness of the result might still cause a swoon.

Try to use a slim variety of eggplant, long or short does not matter. This makes a good party dish, as it tastes even better when left to stand for a few hours.

SERVES *4*

PREPARATION *30 minutes*

COOKING *about 1¼ hours*

Calories per serving *230*
Total fat *High*
Saturated fat *Low*
Protein *Low*
Carbohydrate *Low*
Cholesterol *None*
Vitamins *A, B₁, B₃, B₆, Folate, E*
Minerals *Potassium, Iron, Zinc*

4 EGGPLANTS, TOTAL WEIGHT ABOUT 2¼ POUNDS
4 TABLESPOONS OLIVE OIL
12 OUNCES ONIONS, FINELY CHOPPED
5-6 GARLIC CLOVES, PEELED AND CRUSHED
1 POUND TOMATOES, FINELY CHOPPED
FEW SPRIGS OF FRESH THYME AND MARJORAM,
COARSELY CHOPPED, PLUS MORE FOR GARNISH
3-4 TABLESPOONS FINELY CHOPPED PARSLEY
SALT AND FRESHLY GROUND BLACK PEPPER
1 RED BELL PEPPER
2 TABLESPOONS TOMATO PASTE, DILUTED IN 1¼ CUPS
HOT WATER

1 Preheat the oven to 375°F and lightly oil a baking sheet. If the eggplants still have their stalks on, try to keep them intact for decorative effect. Slit each eggplant lengthwise to open out like a pouch. Lay the eggplants on the baking sheet, slit side down. Brush a little oil on each eggplant and bake for 30 minutes. Take them out of the oven, but keep the oven on with the temperature reduced to 350°F.

2 While the eggplants are baking, prepare the tomato sauce: put the onions in a frying pan with 3-4 tablespoons of water and bring to a simmer. Once the water has evaporated, add the remaining oil and sauté the onion until it just turns a light gold color. Add the garlic and stir for a few seconds. Then add the tomatoes and herbs, reserving a few sprigs of each herb for garnish. Season with salt and pepper and cook gently for 20 minutes, until the sauce looks well amalgamated and quite dry.

3 While the sauce is cooking, scorch the red pepper over a naked flame for a few minutes. Peel it, cut it in half, and deseed it. Then cut the flesh into long strips. Set these aside.

4 Arrange the eggplants side by side in a baking dish that is just large enough to hold them snugly in a single layer, this time with the slit side upward. Sprinkle some salt and pepper over them and then fill each eggplant with the tomato sauce, distributing it evenly. Lay the pepper ribbons diagonally over the stuffing. Pour the diluted tomato paste into the bottom of the dish and bake for 45 minutes, basting the eggplants occasionally. Garnish with the reserved herbs.

Imam Bayildi

FENNEL GRATIN WITH OIL AND CHEESE

Finocchio—*Florence fennel—is an undervalued vegetable with a cool, elegant flavor. Although it is often served raw in salads and its refreshing effects are undoubted, in Italy it is occasionally served cooked, and I am always freshly surprised by its finesse and deliciousness. When cooked, its sweet taste and anise aromas are better projected if it is complemented by a softer texture. It makes an ideal partner for fish, particularly grilled.*

SERVES 4

PREPARATION *about 10 minutes*

COOKING *about 35 minutes*

Calories per serving *146*
Total fat *High*
Saturated fat *Medium*
Protein *Medium*
Carbohydrate *Low*
Cholesterol *8 mg*
Vitamins *B₁, B₆, Folate*
Minerals *Calcium, Potassium, Iron, Zinc*

4 FENNEL BULBS
2½ TABLESPOONS OLIVE OIL
1 TABLESPOON FENNEL SEEDS

¼ TEASPOON COARSE SEA SALT
3 TABLESPOONS FRESHLY GRATED PARMESAN CHEESE
2 TABLESPOONS TOASTED BREADCRUMBS

1 Preheat the oven to 375°F and lightly oil a small gratin dish. Slice off and discard the feathery tops of the fennel. Trim and discard the thick base. If the fennel is bruised or dried up, remove and discard its outer layer. Slice each bulb in two lengthwise.
2 Bring a saucepan of water to a boil, add the fennel pieces, and boil for 4-6 minutes, until they are softer but still with a little resistance in them. Drain them in a colander and then

place them closely together in the prepared gratin dish.
3 Heat the remaining olive oil gently in a small frying pan, add the fennel seeds, and swirl them around for 1 minute until they start to sizzle. Drizzle the oil and seeds over the fennel and then sprinkle the salt, cheese, and breadcrumbs over the top, in that order.
4 Bake on the upper shelf of the oven for 20 minutes, until lightly brown on top.

BAKED EGGPLANT WITH MOZZARELLA

This is a very easy dish, loved by all. Its simplicity makes it the ideal standby. It is based on a dish served to us by my friend the writer Gillian Riley, who is an expert on Italian food. It can be served hot or at room temperature, with a salad and an interesting bread such as ciabatta, or French baguette.

SERVES 4

PREPARATION *20 minutes*

COOKING *25-35 minutes*

1 POUND EGGPLANT (2 MEDIUM EGGPLANTS)
2 TABLESPOONS OLIVE OIL
1 TABLESPOON SUNFLOWER OIL
2 GARLIC CLOVES, PEELED AND CRUSHED
1 TEASPOON DRIED MARJORAM
½ TEASPOON DRIED THYME

SALT AND FRESHLY GROUND BLACK PEPPER

FOR THE TOPPING:
4 OUNCES BUFFALO MOZZARELLA CHEESE, CUT INTO ½-INCH DICE
8 OUNCES TOMATOES, THINLY SLICED

1 Preheat the oven to 400°F. Cut the eggplants into round slices about ¼ inch thick. Mix the remaining ingredients in a bowl. Dip the slices of eggplant in the bowl one at a time to coat lightly, and arrange closely in a single layer in a large roasting pan. If you cannot fit them all in, cook the eggplant slices in 2 batches. Bake for 10 minutes.

2 Take the eggplants out of the oven and lower the oven setting to 375°F. Top each eggplant slice with a slice of tomato and 3-4 mozzarella pieces. Return to the oven and bake for 15 more minutes.

3 Take the eggplant out of the oven and immediately transfer to a flat platter to prevent it from absorbing any more oil.

Calories per serving *185*
Total fat *High*
Saturated fat *High*
Protein *Medium*
Carbohydrate *Low*
Cholesterol *19 mg*
Vitamins *A, B12, C, E*
Minerals *Calcium, Potassium*

CAPONATA
Sicilian Eggplants in Sweet-and-Sour Sauce

Sicilian caponata *bears the hallmarks of its Arab ancestry in its fusion of sweet and sour tastes. However, this fusion should be balanced so that the* caponata *does not lose its charm. Make sure it does not taste predominantly sour, so taste first and then add any extra vinegar if you wish. Traditionally the eggplants are first fried and then added to the dish. However, this version produces lighter results.*

3 TABLESPOONS OLIVE OIL
1 LARGE ONION, PEELED AND SLICED FINELY
1 TEASPOON DRIED OREGANO
2 POUNDS EGGPLANT, DICED SMALL
2 YOUNG CELERY STALKS, CHOPPED
1 POUND TOMATOES, SKINNED AND CHOPPED, OR ONE
14-OUNCE CAN OF CHOPPED TOMATOES

1 TEASPOON DEMERARA SUGAR
½ CUP GREEN OLIVES, RINSED AND PITTED
3 TABLESPOONS CAPERS, RINSED
2-3 TABLESPOONS RED WINE VINEGAR
2 TABLESPOONS PINE NUTS, TOASTED IN A DRY FRYING PAN
FRESHLY GROUND BLACK PEPPER

SERVES 6

PREPARATION
30 minutes

COOKING
45 minutes, plus cooling

Calories per serving *165*
Total fat *High*
Saturated fat *Low*
Protein *Low*
Carbohydrate *Low*
Cholesterol *None*
Vitamins *A, B1, B3, B6, Folate, C, E*
Minerals *Potassium, Iron, Zinc*

1 Heat the oil gently in a heavy-based saucepan and sauté the onion in it until light golden. Add the oregano and eggplant and keep turning with a spatula for 5-10 minutes until they wilt a little.

2 Add only 2 tablespoons of the vinegar at this stage. Add the remaining ingredients except the pine nuts. Cover and simmer for 35-40 minutes, until everything is soft.

3 Taste and adjust the seasoning, adding more vinegar if necessary for a sweet-and-sour balance. Serve the caponata at room temperature, scattering the toasted nuts over it at the last minute.

FRESH PEAS AND ZUCCHINI

This is a simple vegetable dish, but when the vegetables are in season the combination can be astounding. The stars of the show are the peas, and there is no alternative to freshly shelled. Choose young small zucchini, if you can find them, but you could use tiny carrots or small new potatoes instead. This dish can be prepared in advance—even the day before—and served at room temperature.

12 OUNCES (IDEALLY SMALL) ZUCCHINI, INCLUDING THEIR FLOWERS IF STILL ATTACHED
6 SCALLIONS, COARSELY CHOPPED
3-4 TABLESPOONS FRUITY OLIVE OIL
3 POUNDS FRESH PEAS, SHELLED (SHELLED WEIGHT ABOUT 1½ POUNDS)

8 OUNCES (3-4) TOMATOES, SKINNED, DESEEDED, AND DICED
⅔ CUP (APPROXIMATELY) HOT WATER
SALT AND FRESHLY GROUND BLACK PEPPER
2 TABLESPOONS FRESH DILL, COARSELY CHOPPED

1 Keep the zucchini whole if small; if large, quarter them lengthwise.
2 Sauté the scallions in the oil (reserving 1 tablespoon) until glistening, add the peas and tomatoes and stir for 2-3 minutes.
3 Add the water with some seasonings. Cover and simmer for 10 minutes. Add the zucchini and a little more water if needed, as all the vegetables should be submerged in the sauce. Cook gently for 30-35 minutes more, shaking the pan occasionally. Sprinkle in the dill and cook for a few minutes more.
4 Turn out on a serving platter, drizzle the last tablespoonful of oil on top and serve.

SERVES *4*

PREPARATION *30 minutes*

COOKING *about 1 hour*

Calories per serving *317*
Total fat *Medium*
Saturated fat *Medium*
Protein *Medium*
Carbohydrate *Low*
Cholesterol *None*
Vitamins *A, B1, B6, C, E, Folate*
Minerals *Calcium, Potassium, Iron, Zinc*

CATALAN SPINACH

This is a Moorish leftover in the Catalan culinary book. It can accompany poultry or meat dishes, but may also be served as part of the larger mezze *table.*

2 POUNDS SPINACH, COARSELY CHOPPED
2 TABLESPOONS OLIVE OIL
3 TABLESPOONS TOASTED PINE NUTS

3 TABLESPOONS RAISINS, SOAKED IN WARM WATER FOR 10 MINUTES AND RINSED
SALT AND FRESHLY GROUND BLACK PEPPER

1 Place the spinach in a large saucepan over gentle heat and keep stirring so that it all comes in touch with the hot base and wilts. Add a little salt and, once the spinach looks wilted and it has exuded enough moisture, cover the saucepan and let it steam for 5-7 minutes until soft. Drain in a colander.
2 Heat the oil in the saucepan, add the drained spinach, pine nuts, raisins and some black pepper and sauté for 5 more minutes, stirring occasionally and keeping an eye on it. It should be dry but moist by the end.

SERVES *4*

PREPARATION *20 minutes*

COOKING *about 15 minutes*

Calories per serving *188*
Total fat *High*
Saturated fat *Low*
Protein *Medium*
Carbohydrate *Low*
Cholesterol *None*
Vitamins *A, B₁, B₂, B₃, B₆, Folate, C, E*
Minerals *Calcium, Iron, Zinc, Potassium*

Fresh Peas and Zucchini

GLOBE ARTICHOKES WITH FRESH FAVA BEANS

With the first rays of spring sun, the street markets in Greece present mounds of beautiful green artichokes. A little later on the elegant slim fava beans appear, to be followed by the young fresh peas. So inevitably these vegetables are bubbling away in different combinations in every home in the spring.

SERVES *4 as a main course, or 6 as a first course*

PREPARATION *about 40 minutes*

COOKING *about 1 hour*

Calories per serving *200*
Total fat *High*
Saturated fat *Low*
Protein *High*
Carbohydrate *Low*
Cholesterol *None*
Vitamins *A, B₃, B₆, Folate, E*
Minerals *Potassium, Iron, Zinc*

3 POUNDS FRESH FAVA BEANS IN THEIR PODS OR
1 POUND 2 OUNCES FROZEN BEANS, DEFROSTED
4-6 MEDIUM-SIZED GLOBE ARTICHOKES
2 LEMONS
1 LARGE ONION, THINLY SLICED
4 TABLESPOONS OLIVE OIL

1¾ CUPS HOT WATER
SALT AND FRESHLY GROUND BLACK PEPPER
4-5 SCALLIONS, CHOPPED
1 RED BELL PEPPER, DESEEDED AND DICED
LARGE HANDFUL OF FRESH DILL, FINELY CHOPPED

1 Shell the fava beans, discarding the larger pods but keeping some of the smaller younger ones. Trim these all the way around as you would do with large green beans and then cut them in half. Immerse them in a bowl of water, rinse carefully, and drain.

2 Prepare the artichokes by discarding three-quarters or more of their outer leaves until you have reached the tender inner ones. Cut the stem down, leaving about 2 inches attached. Trim off the upper section of the leaves and discard, leaving a short collar around the heart of the artichoke. Cut the artichoke in half lengthwise. You will see in the middle a hairy choke that should be extracted with a stainless-steel spoon or knife and discarded. Now trim the stem and the outer base of the artichoke of its hard dark green skin. Have ready a bowl of water with the juice of half a lemon in it; drop in each artichoke half as you finish it.

3 In a wide-based saucepan, sauté the onion in the hot oil until glistening and add the fava beans. Stir for a few minutes, then add the juice from the remaining 1½ lemons and the hot water. Once it comes to a boil, add the artichoke halves and shake the saucepan to fit everything neatly in it. Add some salt and pepper, cover, and cook gently for 25 minutes. (Do not stir or you may separate the artichokes.)

4 Turn the artichokes over carefully and add the scallions, the red pepper, the dill, and a little more water if needed. Rotate the saucepan and tilt to distribute things evenly, then cover and cook for another 20-25 minutes, until the beans and their pods are quite soft.

5 Serve with fresh bread and a plate of fresh greenery, such as some of the reserved raw younger fava bean pods, additional scallions, arugula, sprigs of parsley, dill, or whatever is on hand.

Globe Artichokes with Fresh Fava Beans

OKRA WITH DRIED LIMES

Okra is loved all over the eastern Mediterranean and is often cooked in casseroles, usually with meat or chicken. In Egypt they add a number of spices to okra dishes; I have also added dried limes (see page 19) which are a favorite ingredient in Iran and the Gulf countries. With their aromatic sourness, they contribute a deep note to the overall taste. They may be removed from the finished dish, but offer them to aficionados, who like to suck them. If you can't find dried limes, some fresh lime juice will still give a delicious result.

This dish works well served with Tabbouleh (page 145), Tahinosalata (page 46) or Baked Eggplant with Mozzarella (page 114).

SERVES *4*

PREPARATION
10 minutes

COOKING
about 1 hour

Calories per serving *184*
Total fat *Low*
Saturated fat *Low*
Protein *Medium*
Carbohydrate *Low*
Cholesterol *None*
Vitamins *A, B₁, B₆, C, E,*
Folate
Minerals *Calcium, Iron,*
Zinc, Potassium

2¼ POUNDS OKRA
3 TABLESPOONS OLIVE OIL
1 LARGE ONION, FINELY CHOPPED
1-2 DRIED CHILIES
3 GARLIC CLOVES, MINCED
1 TABLESPOON GROUND CORIANDER SEEDS

14-OUNCE CAN OF CHOPPED TOMATOES
3 DRIED LIMES, OR 2 TABLESPOONS FRESH LIME JUICE
SALT AND FRESHLY GROUND BLACK PEPPER
HANDFUL OF FRESH CILANTRO LEAVES, COARSELY CHOPPED

1 Trim off and discard the okra tops (see page 14), rinse the okra gently in cold water, and drain.

2 Heat the oil in a large saucepan, add the onion, and stir until light golden. Add the chilies, garlic, and ground coriander, and sauté for a minute or two.

3 Add the tomatoes with their liquid. Once the liquid starts to bubble, add the okra, limes or lime juice, and seasoning. Shake the pan to distribute the ingredients evenly, Cover and cook gently for 30 minutes. If you are using the dried limes, press them with a wooden spoon from time to time to encourage them to give up their flavor.

4 Add the fresh cilantro and cook for 10 minutes more.

Okra with Dried Limes

MOROCCAN STUFFED TOMATOES AND PEPPERS

The practice of stuffing vegetables originated in the Middle East and in Persia. The Ottomans were also very keen on them, but stuffed vegetables must have found their way to North Africa via the Arabs, and, although the dish is not as common there as in Middle Eastern countries and Greece, it is found occasionally in grand buffets in Morocco. In the Hotel Mamounia in Marrakech we have had an exotic version, which was made quite sweet with the addition of dried fruit and was redolent of the warm aroma of cinnamon. In Anatolia in Turkey, it is not only vegetables but also fruits such as quinces or apples that are stuffed. This is probably an influence from Persia. Also in Anatolia, instead of rice stuffings, vegetables may contain cracked wheat and/or chickpeas. There are endless variations in stuffings, with or without meat.

Every summer we had delicious stuffed vegetables at home made by my grandmother, who lived in Smyrna until 1922 when the expulsion of the Greeks took place. These looked like an exotic tapestry, arranged in their large roasting pan before being taken to the local baker where things were routinely baked, as households did not possess ovens at that time. We always had a selection of all the summer vegetables, which included not only tomatoes and green bell peppers but also zucchini and elongated purple eggplants. When you are embarking on the making of such a dish it is worth stuffing some extra vegetables—say, an extra tomato and a pepper—as they are so popular.

SERVES *4*

PREPARATION *about 1 hour*

COOKING *about 1 hour*

Calories per serving *685*
Total fat *High*
Saturated fat *Low*
Protein *Low*
Carbohydrate *Low*
Cholesterol *None*
Vitamins *A, B₁, B₂, B₃, B₆, Folate, C, E*
Minerals *Calcium, Iron, Zinc, Potassium*

4 LARGE TOMATOES
4 LARGE GREEN BELL PEPPERS
½ TEASPOON SUGAR
2 TABLESPOONS TOASTED BREADCRUMBS (2 SLICES OF TOASTED BREAD PUT THROUGH A FOOD PROCESSOR)

FOR THE STUFFING:
4 TABLESPOONS OLIVE OIL
2 LARGE ONIONS, THINLY SLICED
¾-INCH PIECE OF FRESH GINGERROOT, PEELED AND GRATED
¼ TEASPOON GROUND ALLSPICE (OR 4 GRAINS OF IT)
2 SMALL CINNAMON STICKS
½ CUP LONG-GRAIN RICE, RINSED
8 OUNCES DRIED APRICOTS, COARSELY CHOPPED

2 OUNCES DATES, PITTED AND CHOPPED (OPTIONAL)
JUICE OF ½ LEMON
⅔ CUP HOT WATER
LARGE HANDFUL OF FRESH PARSLEY, FINELY CHOPPED
HANDFUL OF FRESH CILANTRO, CHOPPED
4-5 SPRIGS OF MINT, CHOPPED
½ CUP PINE NUTS, TOASTED LIGHTLY
½ CUP FLAKED ALMONDS, TOASTED LIGHTLY
2 TABLESPOONS CURRANTS, RINSED
SALT AND FRESHLY GROUND BLACK PEPPER

FOR THE SAUCE:
8 OUNCES TOMATOES, SKINNED AND FINELY CHOPPED
2 TABLESPOONS OLIVE OIL
⅔ CUP HOT WATER

1 Preheat the oven to 350°F. Cut a round slice off the top (stem end) of each of the 4 large tomatoes and set aside. Do the same with the peppers. Scoop most of the tomato flesh out with a teaspoon, chop it finely and set aside. Place the tomatoes upside down for about 5 minutes to allow excess moisture to drain off. Keep all their juices. Trim and deseed the peppers.

2 Prepare the stuffing: heat the oil in a saucepan or large frying pan and sauté the onion until light golden. Add the ginger and spices and mix them in for 1-2 minutes, until aromatic. Add the drained rice and sauté for a few minutes until well coated in the oil and the spices. Add the reserved tomato flesh and juices, the dried fruit, lemon juice and hot water. Let it simmer for 5 minutes until most of the liquid has been absorbed. Withdraw from the heat, remove the cinnamon, and mix in the remaining ingredients. Season.

3 Place the prepared tomatoes and peppers closely together, standing up side by side, in a small roasting pan. Sprinkle a pinch of sugar inside each tomato and fill them up loosely with the stuffing. Do not press it down, so that it has room to expand. Fill the peppers in the same way and seal the tomatoes and peppers with their respective tops.

4 Mix the sauce ingredients in a small bowl and pour over the top and around the vegetables. Cook in the oven for 50 minutes, basting the vegetables from time to time.

5 Turn the oven up to 400°F, sprinkle the breadcrumbs on top and bake for 15-20 more minutes, until the top browns.

Overleaf: Moroccan Stuffed Tomatoes and Peppers and Dolmathes (page 126)

DOLMATHES
Stuffed Grape Leaves

Dolmathes *are among the best dishes in Greek cooking. These small parcels, filled with the aromas of the fields, represent the essence of spring with their captivating tastes.*

Under the name of thria *they have been a favorite in Greece for some time, approximately two thousand years.* Thria *in ancient Greek meant "fig leaves," but at least by the fifth century* B.C. *it also meant a dish of stuffed fig leaves, as they were mentioned in Aristophanes'* Knights *and* The Frogs, *according to classicist Andrew Dalby. Soon the Greeks discovered that grape leaves made a more tasty alternative. So by the fifth century* A.D. *the definition given by lexicographers is: "Fig or grape leaves; also foodstuffs wrapped in these." So much for historical continuity.*

This is a laborious dish to make, so try to enlist some help. In Greece it is often the result of a joint effort of extended families, friends and neighbors. Grape leaves are stuffed with various ingredients all over the Middle East and Turkey, but I think the best versions are made in Greece.

Fresh grape leaves—ideally young ones picked at the beginning of the season—produce the best results. Alternatively, one can buy packets of preserved leaves. If you have access to a grape vine, you can freeze its leaves in season. Stack them in piles of a dozen, roll them up, cover with plastic wrap, and place in the freezer. Let them thaw at room temperature for two hours before use. (See previous pages.)

MAKES *about 40*

PREPARATION
about 1 hour

COOKING
about 1 hour

Calories *30 each*
Total fat *High*
Saturated fat *Low*
Protein *Low*
Carbohydrate *Low*
Cholesterol *None*
Vitamins *A*
Minerals *Potassium, Iron*

8 OUNCES GRAPE LEAVES (45-48)

1 TABLESPOON FINELY CHOPPED DILL, TO SERVE

1-2 LEMONS, CUT INTO WEDGES, TO SERVE

FOR THE STUFFING:

HEAPING ½ CUP LONG-GRAIN RICE, RINSED AND DRAINED

12 OUNCES ONIONS, FINELY CHOPPED

3 TABLESPOONS PINE NUTS, LIGHTLY TOASTED

2 TABLESPOONS DARK OR GOLDEN RAISINS, RINSED (OPTIONAL)

4-5 TABLESPOONS FINELY CHOPPED FRESH DILL

4 TABLESPOONS FINELY CHOPPED PARSLEY

3 TABLESPOONS COARSELY CHOPPED FRESH MINT

JUICE OF 1 LEMON

4 TABLESPOONS OLIVE OIL

HOT WATER

SALT AND FRESHLY GROUND BLACK PEPPER

1 Rinse fresh leaves and blanch them in batches of 6-8 in a saucepan of lightly salted boiling water for 1 minute, or less if they are young. Take them out with a slotted spatula and drain. They should be just wilted and not cooked. If using preserved leaves—which are very salty—rinse them first and plunge them in a bowl of boiling water for 5 minutes. Take out and place in a bowl of cold water, then rinse them again and place in a strainer.

2 Mix all the stuffing ingredients together in a bowl, using only half of the oil and lemon juice at this stage.

3 Line the base of a wide saucepan or sauté pan with some of the grape leaves. Trim the stalks of the others and spread each leaf on a plate, uneven side upward. If the leaf is small take a teaspoon of stuffing (if large use a tablespoonful), and place it along the stem end of the leaf. Press the stuffing into an elongated sausage-like shape and fold the stem end of the leaf over it. Next, fold the two edges of the leaf inward and roll tightly to the end into a small cigar shape. Squeeze the rolled package in your hand to get rid of excess moisture if they appear too wet.

4 Arrange the rolls tightly in circles around the base of the pan, trapping their loose ends underneath. When one layer is formed sprinkle with a little seasoning and start another layer on top. It is best not to have more than 3 layers, otherwise you get the bottom ones overcooked and squashed. Drizzle with the remaining oil and lemon juice, and then place a small inverted plate on top to keep them in place while cooking.

5 Slowly pour in 2 cups of hot water, cover, and simmer for 50 minutes. Try one, and if the rice is too crunchy cook a little longer.

6 The dolmathes are delicious served hot or cold. Arrange on a pretty platter, sprinkle the dill on top, and surround with lemon wedges.

FAVA BEANS WITH CHARD

This earthy-flavored Middle Eastern dish—usually made by my friend Sami Zubaida, one of the best cooks around—has an instant appeal for everyone around the table. The dish is infinitely better when made in the fall with the summer's crop, before the beans hit middle age.

10 OUNCES WHOLE DRIED BROAD BEANS, SOAKED OVERNIGHT

3 TABLESPOONS OLIVE OIL

1 TABLESPOON GROUND CUMIN

1 TEASPOON GROUND CORIANDER SEEDS

1 POUND SWISS CHARD, TRIMMED OF STALKS AND COARSELY CHOPPED

JUICE OF 1-2 LEMONS, ACCORDING TO TASTE

SALT AND FRESHLY GROUND BLACK PEPPER

SERVES *4*

PREPARATION *10-15 minutes, plus overnight soaking*

COOKING *1¼-1¾ hours*

Calories per serving *271*
Total fat *Medium*
Saturated fat *Low*
Protein *High*
Carbohydrate *Low*
Cholesterol *None*
Vitamins *A, B₁, B₂, B₃, B₆, Folate, C*
Minerals *Calcium, Potassium, Iron, Zinc*

1 Rinse the beans, cover with plenty of fresh water, and boil until quite tender. This could take between 1 and 1½ hours, according to their age. Discard any skins that come off in the process. Drain, reserving 2 cupfuls of the cooking liquid.

2 Heat the oil in a sauté pan, add the spices and swirl them around for a minute until their aroma rises. Add the chard and sauté, turning it around with a spatula. Add half of the reserved cooking liquid with some seasoning. Cover and simmer gently for about 10-15 minutes, until soft.

3 Place the drained beans in a large bowl, add the cooked Swiss chard with some more seasoning and the lemon juice, and toss to mix everything. It should be quite moist, almost soupy, so add a little more of the reserved cooking liquid if necessary.

4 Bowls of black olives and little plates of flat-leaved parsley on the stalk and arugula, and little scarlet radishes go well with this dish.

PUY LENTILS WITH DILL, SALSA VERDE, AND ROAST PEPPERS

Puy lentils are the aristocrats among lentils. They are small, with a silvery-green coat and light green insides. However small and insignificant they may look, once cooked they hold their shape better than other lentils and their flavor is high up on the culinary scale. Of course not all Puy lentils in the market are the genuine article; that is, they don't necessarily come from the town of Le Puy in the Auvergne. A lot are Puy-style lentils grown elsewhere in France or in other European countries, but they are still better than the large green lentils, which are tasteless and disintegrate easily. This is the most delicious lentil recipe and it has evolved after numerous trials.

SERVES *4 people as a main course, or 6 as a first course*

PREPARATION *about 20 minutes, plus cooling*

COOKING *40-50 minutes*

Calories per serving *376*
Total fat *Low*
Saturated fat *Low*
Protein *High*
Carbohydrate *Medium*
Cholesterol *None*
Vitamins *A, B₁, B₂, B₃, B₆, Folate, C, E*
Minerals *Calcium, Potassium, Iron, Zinc, Selenium*

4 RED BELL PEPPERS, RINSED AND DRIED
1 POUND PUY OR SIMILAR SMALL LENTILS, PICKED CLEAN AND RINSED
SALT AND FRESHLY GROUND BLACK PEPPER
LARGE HANDFUL OF FRESH DILL, COARSELY CHOPPED

FOR THE SALSA VERDE:
2 FRESH GREEN CHILIES, DESEEDED AND CHOPPED

3 GARLIC CLOVES, MINCED
½ IN-PIECE OF FRESH GINGERROOT, PEELED AND GRATED
LARGE HANDFUL OF FLAT-LEAVED PARSLEY, CHOPPED
SMALL HANDFUL OF FRESH DILL, CHOPPED
1 TEASPOON DIJON MUSTARD
JUICE OF 1½ LEMONS
3 TABLESPOONS OLIVE OIL

1 Preheat the oven to 375°F. Cover a baking sheet with foil, lay the peppers on it, and roast them for 35-40 minutes, turning them over once about halfway through. Remove them from the oven and when they are cool enough to handle, peel, trim, and deseed them. Keep one pepper aside for the salsa and cut the rest into small dice.

2 Cover the lentils with cold water, bring to a boil, and drain. Cover them with fresh water, bring to a boil, and simmer very briefly, keeping an eye on them. They will take 7-9 minutes, as they should still be a little hard. Drain and empty them into a large bowl. Add some seasoning, the diced peppers, and the dill, and mix well.

3 To make the salsa, place all the ingredients apart from the oil in a food processor, add the reserved roast pepper, and process with short bursts until everything has the consistency of crumbs. With the machine still running, add the olive oil, dribbling it in slowly until it all looks well amalgamated.

4 A couple of hours before they are to be served, coat the lentils with this salsa so that all the exotic flavors have a chance to permeate the lentils. Garnish with some reserved dill and parsley sprigs.

Puy Lentils with Dill, Salsa Verde, and Roast Peppers

CHICKPEA AND SPINACH CASSEROLE

On the whole, chickpeas are neglected in the West; not so in the Middle East, where they appear transformed in a hundred guises. There is no mezze *table without the sharply appetizing* hummus *of the Arab countries and Turkey, and in most of the Mediterranean countries chickpeas are also made into wonderful casseroles and soups, in combination with spices, vegetables, or meat.*

This recipe was first described to me in the middle 1960s by a Cypriot shoemaker in North London's Chapel Market, and an almost identical one is made all over Cyprus using black-eyed peas.

SERVES *4-6 as a main course*

PREPARATION
20 minutes, plus overnight soaking

COOKING
about 2¼ hours

Calories per serving *354*
Total fat *Medium*
Saturated fat *Low*
Protein *Medium*
Carbohydrate *Low*
Cholesterol *None*
Vitamins *A, B₁, B₂, B₃, B₆,*
Folate, C, E
Minerals *Calcium,*
Potassium, Iron, Zinc

12 OUNCES CHICKPEAS, PICKED CLEAN AND SOAKED OVERNIGHT IN COLD WATER

2 LARGE ONIONS, CHOPPED

4 TABLESPOONS OLIVE OIL

1-2 TABLESPOONS GROUND CUMIN

4-5 GARLIC CLOVES, MINCED

1 LEMON

1 POUND FRESH SPINACH, OR 10-OUNCE PACKET OF FROZEN LEAF SPINACH, THAWED

SALT AND FRESHLY GROUND BLACK PEPPER

1 Drain and rinse the chickpeas. In a large pan, cover them with plenty of fresh water and bring to a boil. Skim, cover, and cook until they are soft. This could take about 1 hour or more (if using a pressure cooker, about 20 minutes). Drain, reserving the liquid.

2 Using the same saucepan, sauté the chopped onions in the hot oil until glistening and add the ground cumin and the minced garlic. When they become aromatic, add the cooked chick-peas and enough of their cooking liquid barely to cover them. Add the lemon juice,

cover and simmer for about 1 hour.

3 Toward the end of that time, if using fresh spinach rinse it, drain, and chop coarsely. Add the spinach, salt and a generous amount of pepper to the casserole. Mix well and cook for a further 15-20 minutes, or a little less if using frozen spinach.

4 This dish actually improves with standing, so it can be cooked the day before. It may also be served at room temperature. Serve it with Sarimsakli Yogurt, the garlicky Turkish yogurt sauce (page 33).

Top: Chickpea and Spinach Casserole; bottom: Fava (page 132)

MAGHREBI LENTILS WITH CHERMOULA

Lentils can be transformed from the humble ingredient they are to royal status with the addition of a few aromatic ingredients. With their nutty flavor accentuated with garlic, spices and herbs, and given the speed with which they can be prepared, they make the most delicious standby dishes. In Morocco, chermoula sauce is often used as a marinade for fish. This dish can be served with any grilled meats or fish, or by itself with Turkish Muhammara (page 42) or Tahinosalata (46) and fresh bread.

SERVES *4*

PREPARATION *20 minutes*

COOKING *about 20 minutes, plus cooling*

Calories per serving *301*
Total fat *Medium*
Saturated fat *Low*
Protein *High*
Carbohydrate *Low*
Cholesterol *None*
Vitamins *A, B₁, B₂, B₃, B₆, Folate, C*
Minerals *Iron, Zinc, Selenium, Potassium*

10 OUNCES SMALL BROWN-GREEN LENTILS, RINSED
2 BAY LEAVES

FOR THE CHERMOULA SAUCE:
3 TABLESPOONS OLIVE OIL
1 FRESH CHILI, DESEEDED AND FINELY CHOPPED
1 TABLESPOON GROUND CUMIN
1 TABLESPOON PAPRIKA

1 TEASPOON GROUND CORIANDER
¼ TEASPOON GROUND CINNAMON
3 GARLIC CLOVES, PEELED AND CRUSHED
4 TABLESPOONS EACH COARSELY CHOPPED CILANTRO AND FLAT-LEAVED PARSLEY
3 TABLESPOONS FRESH MINT, FINELY CHOPPED
SALT AND FRESHLY GROUND BLACK PEPPER
JUICE OF 1 OR 2 LEMONS

1 Rinse the lentils, cover with fresh water, add the bay leaves, and bring to a boil. Simmer gently for 15-20 minutes. The lentils should be soft enough to eat, but still intact and a little firm. Drain and discard the bay leaves.
2 Make the sauce: heat the oil gently in a sauté pan and sauté the chili and spices briefly for about 1 minute. Add the garlic, and as soon as it becomes aromatic, add the lentils and stir to coat them in the sauce. Add the herbs and some seasoning, stir for a further minute, and then withdraw from the heat.
3 Let the mixture cool a little before serving. Add the juice of 1 lemon first, taste, and adjust accordingly (it should be quite sharp-tasting). Serve either warm or at room temperature.

FAVA
Yellow Split Pea Purée

SERVES *4*

PREPARATION *about 20 minutes, plus 1 hour's soaking*

COOKING *about 1 hour*

If you ask any Greek, they will tell you that fava *is the dish that sustained them in the frugal years after the war. However,* fava *goes back even longer than that—perhaps a couple of thousand years—as it is the kind of dish that was popular in classical Greece. A very similar-sounding dish called* etnos *was sold in the streets of Athens and, according to Aristophanes, it was a favorite of Hercules. Although neglected during the affluent 1970s and 1980s, it has made a triumphant return, acknowledged as one of those dishes that make up the basic fabric of healthy Mediterranean food. Greek* fava *are smaller than ordinary yellow split peas, have a sweeter taste, and are not as solid. (See previous pages.)*

8 OUNCES **G**REEK FAVA, OR **5** OUNCES YELLOW
SPLIT PEAS
1 SMALL ONION, FINELY CHOPPED
2-3 SMALL RED ONIONS, THINLY SLICED
2-3 TABLESPOONS OLIVE OIL

JUICE OF 1 LEMON
1 TABLESPOON FINELY CHOPPED PARSLEY
4-5 BLACK OLIVES
SALT AND FRESHLY GROUND BLACK PEPPER
1 LEMON, QUARTERED, TO SERVE

Calories per serving *197*
Total fat *Medium*
Saturated fat *Low*
Protein *Medium*
Carbohydrate *Low*
Cholesterol *None*
Vitamins *B₁, B₃, Folate, E*
Minerals *Iron, Zinc, Potassium*

1 Pick the peas clean of grit and soak them in cold water for about 1 hour. Rinse several times, place in a heavy-based pan, and add 4½ cups of water. Bring to a boil and skim until clear.
2 Add the onion and simmer uncovered for 45-50 minutes, stirring occasionally. Add salt toward the end of cooking time. When the split peas appear mushy toward the end, keep an eye on them as they may stick. Taste to make sure they are properly cooked; if not,

add a little extra water. Once cooked, the mixture should look soupy.
3 Mash it properly with a potato masher or put it through a food processor immediately, while it is still hot, as it solidifies once cold.
4 Spread the purée on a platter before it solidifies and let it cool. Sprinkle the red onions all over the top, followed by some black pepper, olive oil, lemon juice, and chopped parsley. Pile the olives in the center and serve warm or cold with lemon wedges.

MAS PIYAZI
Mung Bean Salad with Fresh Pomegranates

The Turkish dish can also be made with Puy or small brown lentils instead of mung beans.

8 OUNCES MUNG BEANS, PICKED CLEAN AND SOAKED
FOR 2 HOURS
2 POMEGRANATES, PEELED AND SEEDS EXTRACTED,
RESERVING ANY JUICES (SEE PAGE 19)
3 SMALL RED ONIONS OR SHALLOTS, THINLY SLICED
3 SCALLIONS, THINLY SLICED
LARGE HANDFUL OF FLAT-LEAVED PARSLEY, FINELY
CHOPPED

LARGE HANDFUL OF ARUGULA, COARSELY CHOPPED
1 TABLESPOON ANTEP PEPPER (PAGE 15) OR RED
PEPPER FLAKES

FOR THE DRESSING:
5 TABLESPOONS POMEGRANATE SYRUP, DILUTED IN 5
TABLESPOONS WATER, OR THE JUICE OF 1 LEMON
3 TABLESPOONS LIGHT OLIVE OIL OR PEANUT OIL

SERVES *4-6*

PREPARATION *25 minutes, plus 2 hours' soaking*

COOKING *25 minutes*

Calories per serving *242*
Total fat *Medium*
Saturated fat *Low*
Protein *High*
Carbohydrate *Medium*
Cholesterol *None*
Vitamins *A, B₁, B₃, B₆, Folate, C*
Minerals *Potassium, Iron, Zinc*

1 Drain and rinse the mung beans. Cover with fresh water and boil gently until they are tender but not disintegrating (which happens suddenly and rapidly), about 25 minutes. (Lentils will take 10 minutes.)
2 Drain and mix with the remaining

ingredients. Season with salt to taste.
3 Mix the dressing ingredients together, including the reserved pomegranate juices. (If the syrup is too set to pour out, sit the bottle in hot water for 15 minutes.) Pour over the beans and toss gently until well mixed.

Salads

SALADE NIÇOISE

This is a dish with a double identity, like Dr Jekyll and Mr Hyde. It can be sensational or it can be an amalgam of tired leftovers. Every family restaurant in Nice will have a different version of it, all claiming theirs is the most authentic. In my mind there are certain things that have to be included to call it a true salade niçoise. The basics are potatoes (ideally small or new and tasty), tuna (ideally fresh but canned will do), French green beans, tomatoes, canned anchovy filets, olives and, maybe, lettuce. The potatoes respond much better to vinaigrette if they are dressed while they are still hot.

SERVES 4

PREPARATION 25
minutes

COOKING
12-15 minutes

Calories per serving *419*
Total fat *High*
Saturated fat *Low*
Protein *High*
Carbohydrate *Low*
Cholesterol *170 mg*
Vitamins *A, B group, C, E*
Minerals *Calcium,
Potassium, Iron, Zinc,
Selenium, Iodine*

1¼ POUNDS SMALL POTATOES, RINSED

8 OUNCES FRENCH GREEN BEANS, TOPPED, TAILED
AND STEAMED UNTIL JUST TENDER

1 RED BELL PEPPER, TRIMMED, DESEEDED AND SLICED
INTO THIN STRIPS

7-OUNCE CAN OF TUNA IN SUNFLOWER OIL, DRAINED

10 OUNCES TOMATOES, TRIMMED AND CUT INTO
THIN WEDGES

1 LARGE RED ONION, THINLY SLICED

4 CANNED ANCHOVY FILETS, DRAINED AND
FINELY CHOPPED

3 TABLESPOONS CAPERS, RINSED AND DRAINED

HANDFUL OF FLAT-LEAVED PARSLEY, FINELY CHOPPED

2-3 SPRIGS OF BASIL, TORN BY HAND

6-8 SMALL BLACK OLIVES

3 HARD-COOKED EGGS, SHELLED AND QUARTERED

5-6 SMALL CRISP ROMAINE LETTUCE LEAVES
(OPTIONAL)

FOR THE VINAIGRETTE:

3 TABLESPOONS OLIVE OIL

2 TABLESPOONS RED WINE VINEGAR

1 TEASPOON COARSE-GRAIN FRENCH MUSTARD

2 TABLESPOONS LIGHT FRESH FARMER CHEESE

SALT AND FRESHLY GROUND BLACK PEPPER

1 Boil the potatoes in their skins, making sure they are not overcooked. Drain and, when cool enough to handle, peel them and, if they are small, cut them in half lengthwise; if they are larger, cut them into small walnut-sized pieces. Place the potatoes in a large bowl.
2 Beat the vinaigrette ingredients together until smooth, taste and adjust the seasoning if necessary. Coat the potatoes with it while they are still warm. These can now wait for a few

hours, if necessary, covered with plastic wrap.
3 Just before the salad is to be served, add to the bowl the remaining ingredients, except the lettuce, if using, and the eggs. Toss gently to coat everything in the vinaigrette.
4 If you are using lettuce, arrange the leaves on a platter and empty the salad on them. Otherwise, just tip the salad directly on to the platter. Garnish with the hard-cooked egg quarters.

Salade Niçoise

FATTOUSH
Bread and Purslane Salad

This Syrian salad is loved all around the Eastern Mediterranean coast. Bread, particularly stale bread, has always been used ingeniously in Mediterranean countries. The Italian panzanella *is a salad not unlike* fattoush. *Often the bread is toasted and used with soups like the Castilian* sopa de ajo *or the Egyptian* fata. *This variation comes from my friend Sami Zubaida; it is one of the many treats we have had around his large table. The dark red flakes of sumac are a must for the authentic slightly sour tone of this salad.*

SERVES 4

PREPARATION 25-30
*minutes, at least 1
hour before serving*

Calories per serving 211
Total fat *Medium*
Saturated fat *Low*
Protein *Low*
Carbohydrate *Low*
Cholesterol *None*
Vitamins *A, B₁, B₃, B₆,
Folate, C, E*
Minerals *Calcium,
Potassium, Iron*

2 PITA BREADS OR 3 SLICES OF STALE WHITE BREAD
SMALL BUNCH OF PURSLANE OR ARUGULA
1 SMALL GREEN BELL PEPPER
1 SMALL CUCUMBER, RINSED AND FINELY DICED
4-5 SMALL TOMATOES, QUARTERED
3-4 SCALLIONS, CHOPPED
LARGE HANDFUL OF PARSLEY, FINELY CHOPPED
2 TABLESPOONS FINELY CHOPPED FRESH CILANTRO

3 TABLESPOONS FINELY CHOPPED FRESH MINT
1 TABLESPOON SUMAC FLAKES (OPTIONAL)

FOR THE VINAIGRETTE:
JUICE OF 1-2 LEMONS
3 TABLESPOONS OLIVE OIL
2 GARLIC CLOVES, PEELED AND CRUSHED
SALT AND FRESHLY GROUND BLACK PEPPER

1 Toast the bread until crisp and then break it up into small uneven pieces.
2 Trim the purslane or arugula of its thick stalks and coarsely chop the leaves. Trim and deseed the pepper, and cut it into small dice. Place all the salad ingredients in a large bowl.
3 Beat the vinaigrette ingredients together and season. Add this to the bowl and toss the salad to coat everything in the dressing. The moisture from the vegetables and the herbs will help moisten the bread (the original recipe uses much more oil, so feel free to add more if you are not counting calories). However, the dressing is best added at least 1 hour before serving, so that the bread softens and absorbs all the other flavors.

HORIATIKI SALATA

SERVES 4

PREPARATION 15-20
minutes

Calories per serving 177
Total fat *High*
Saturated fat *High*
Protein *Low*

Horiatiki, *meaning simply "peasant style," is a salad now synonymous with Greek summer meals, usually as a prelude to grilled fish or* souvlaki. *It is also substantial enough to make lunch by itself.*

10 OUNCES RIPE TOMATOES
1 MEDIUM RED ONION, QUARTERED
½ GREEN BELL PEPPER, DESEEDED AND SLICED
THINLY IN RIBBONS
SMALL PIECE OF CUCUMBER, THINLY SLICED

6-8 BLACK OLIVES
4 OUNCES GREEK FETA CHEESE, SLICED INTO 4
¼ TEASPOON DRIED OREGANO
3 TABLESPOONS OLIVE OIL
SALT AND FRESHLY GROUND BLACK PEPPER

1 Slice the tomatoes in half and trim off the stalk ends. Slice each half into thick wedges. Slice each onion quarter very thinly.

2 Place all the ingredients, apart from the cheese, oregano and 1 teaspoon of the olive oil, in a bowl. Season to taste, toss gently to mix everything, and coat it in the oil.

3 Place the slices of Feta on top, drizzle the reserved oil on it, and sprinkle the oregano all over. You now have an authentic horiatiki.

Carbohydrate *Low*
Cholesterol *20 mg*
Vitamins *A, B group, C, E*
Minerals *Calcium, Potassium*

MESCLUN WITH GOAT CHEESE

It is only in France and Italy that I have come across a proper mixture of salad greens to deserve the name of the original Provençal mesclun. *The best way to form an idea of what it can be is to visit one of the large Mediterranean markets, such as that in Nice or the Mercato Centrale near the Piazza San Lorenzo in Florence, where the colorful selection is particularly astounding in the fall.*

A mesclun *should include young leaves of both wild and cultivated greens, such as dandelion,* barba di cappuccino *(monk's beard), tiny peppery arugula leaves, lamb's lettuce, purslane, chervil, oak-leaf lettuce and occasionally a number of unrecognizable items seasonal and indigenous to the area. Such items are often sold already mixed as well as separately. Very rarely do we have access to such a glowing array of crisply fresh greenery, but we can improvise. Try to use the crisp inner leaves of different lettuce hearts for the basis of the salad. Arugula leaves are indispensable.*

6 OUNCES MESCLUN OR A VARIETY OF SALAD LEAVES AND HERBS AS ABOVE
3 OUNCES MATURE OR SEMI-MATURE GOAT CHEESE WITH A SHARP TASTE AND CRUMBLY TEXTURE, SUCH AS A CROTTIN

FOR THE VINAIGRETTE:
1 TABLESPOON BALSAMIC VINEGAR
1 TABLESPOON LEMON JUICE
1 SMALL GARLIC CLOVE, CRUSHED
2 TABLESPOONS HAZELNUT OR WALNUT OIL
SALT

SERVES *4*

PREPARATION *10-15 minutes*

Calories per serving *109*
Total fat *Medium*
Saturated fat *Medium*
Protein *Medium*
Carbohydrate *Low*
Cholesterol *20 mg*
Vitamins *B12, Folate*
Minerals *Calcium, Potassium*

1 Place the mixed salad leaves in a bowl and crumble the cheese on top.

2 Beat together all the vinaigrette ingredients, apart from the oil. Then beat in the oil and adjust the seasoning, if necessary. Pour the dressing over the salad and toss well.

Overleaf left to right: Mesclun with Goat Cheese, Black Olive Salad with Pimentón (page 142), Mozzarella with Sun-Dried Tomatoes, Anchovy and Basil (page 142)

MOZZARELLA WITH SUN-DRIED TOMATOES, ANCHOVY, AND BASIL

This easy dish, full of strong, simple flavors makes an ideal standby. (See previous pages.)

SERVES *4*

PREPARATION *10 minutes*

Calories per serving *299*
Total fat *High*
Saturated fat *Medium*
Protein *Low*
Carbohydrate *Low*
Cholesterol *None*
Vitamins *B₃, B₁₂, E*
Minerals *Potassium, Iron, Iodine*

1 BUFFALO MOZZARELLA CHEESE, ABOUT 5 OUNCES
6 PIECES OF SUN-DRIED TOMATOES PRESERVED IN OIL
3 CANNED ANCHOVY FILETS, CUT INTO 3-4 PIECES
12 BLACK OLIVES

SMALL HANDFUL OF BASIL LEAVES
2 TABLESPOONS OLIVE OIL
1 TEASPOON BALSAMIC VINEGAR

1 Slice the mozzarella thinly and arrange the pieces on a pretty platter. Top each slice with a sun-dried tomato and then with 1 or 2 small pieces of anchovy. Sprinkle the olives all over.
2 Beat the oil and vinegar together lightly and sprinkle this all over the salad. Decorate with the basil leaves and serve.

BLACK OLIVE SALAD WITH PIMENTÓN

This is a salad that appears both in Spain—often as tapas*—and in North Africa. It goes well with grilled kebabs and fish, as well as legume dishes, such as the Fava Beans with Chard (page 127) or Chickpea and Spinach Casserole (page 130). (See previous pages.)*

SERVES *4*

PREPARATION *15-20 minutes, plus 1-2 hours' standing*

Calories per serving *140*
Total fat *High*
Saturated fat *Medium*
Protein *Low*
Carbohydrate *Low*
Cholesterol *None*
Vitamins *A, C, E*
Minerals *Potassium, Iron*

2 PURPLE SHALLOTS, OR 1 SMALL RED ONION
10 OUNCES BLACK OLIVES, PITTED AND CHOPPED
1 TABLESPOON SWEET PIMENTÓN (PIMENTÓN DULCE, SEE PAGE 14) OR PAPRIKA
2 TABLESPOONS FINELY CHOPPED PARSLEY
1 LEMON, TO SERVE

FOR THE VINAIGRETTE:
JUICE OF ½ LEMON
1 GARLIC CLOVE, PEELED AND CRUSHED
¼ TEASPOON CUMIN
LARGE PINCH OF CHILI POWDER
2 TABLESPOONS OLIVE OIL

1 Dice or thinly slice the shallots or onions. Place the salad ingredients in a bowl.
2 Lightly beat together all the vinaigrette ingredients, apart from the olive oil. Then beat in the oil gradually.
3 Pour the vinaigrette over the salad and toss to coat everything. Let the salad stand for 1-2 hours so that all the flavors can blend.
4 Empty the salad out on a platter and serve with lemon quarters and garnished with some reserved parsley sprigs. In hot weather it is best served lightly chilled.

ROMAINE WITH ARUGULA AND DILL

This is the salad that I always return to when I am longing for a pure and refreshing taste. It is a salad with no frills, an everyday affair that we commonly had at home in Athens, and which I find intimately familiar. Try to use only the inner young leaves of the lettuce, as they taste sweeter.

1 ROMAINE LETTUCE

LARGE HANDFUL OF YOUNG ARUGULA LEAVES

3 TABLESPOONS FINELY CHOPPED DILL

2-INCH PIECE OF CUCUMBER, THINLY SLICED

2 SCALLIONS, THINLY SLICED

3 TABLESPOONS OLIVE OIL

1-2 TABLESPOONS LEMON JUICE

SALT

SERVES *4*

PREPARATION *15-20 minutes*

Calories per serving *95*
Total fat *High*
Saturated fat *Medium*
Protein *Low*
Carbohydrate *Low*
Cholesterol *None*
Vitamins *Folate, C, E*
Minerals *Potassium, Iron*

1 Trim and discard the outer leaves of the lettuce. Rinse the remaining leaves and dry them well. Place 3-4 leaves on top of each other, roll them together lengthwise and cut the roll across in thin slices, like a chiffonnade. Place the shreds in a bowl.
2 Chop the arugula leaves coarsely and add this to the lettuce, together with the cucumber and scallions.
3 Beat the oil and lemon juice together lightly. Pour this dressing over the salad and toss gently to coat everything in it.
4 Sprinkle the dill over the salad, followed by a little salt, and toss a little more to mix in.

GREEN OLIVE AND POMEGRANATE SALAD

Of the thirty or so dishes that made the sumptuous lunch for us prepared and presented by the ladies of Gaziantep in southeast Turkey, this was the one that impressed me most with its simplicity and novelty. It is obviously a dish of autumn, when the scarlet pomegranates appear unabashedly in mountainous heaps on carts all over Turkey. This is also the time for the fresh crop of juicy green olives and the new tasty walnuts…all ingredients with sensational flavor.

1 CUP WALNUT PIECES

8 OUNCES GREEN OLIVES, PITTED AND CHOPPED

2-3 SCALLIONS, FINELY CHOPPED

3-4 STALKS OF FLAT-LEAVED PARSLEY, FINELY CHOPPED

SEEDS AND JUICE FROM 1 POMEGRANATE (SEE PAGE 19)

3 TABLESPOONS OLIVE OIL

½ TEASPOON URFA PEPPER FLAKES (SEE PAGE 15) OR CHILI FLAKES

SERVES *4*

PREPARATION *15-20 minutes*

COOKING *10 minutes*

Calories per serving *352*
Total fat *High*
Saturated fat *Low*
Protein *Low*
Carbohydrate *Low*
Cholesterol *None*
Vitamins *Folate, E*
Minerals *Iron, Zinc, Potassium, Calcium*

1 Preheat the oven to 325°F. Line a baking sheet with foil and spread the walnuts on it. Bake for 10 minutes. Take out and let the nuts cool, then chop them coarsely in a food processor or bash them with a rolling pin.
2 In a large bowl, combine the chopped nuts with all the other ingredients except the pepper flakes. Mix gently.
3 Spread the salad on a small platter and sprinkle the pepper flakes on top.

TABBOULEH
Lebanese Parsley Salad

When we have tabbouleh in the summer in Greece, my teenage daughter Alexandra complains because she says it is like eating the undergrowth of the surrounding hillsides or the garden … and this is exactly what tabbouleh is. A platter of it is like a synthesis of a kitchen garden, with its aromas, its colors, its different textures, and its multi-layered tastes. It is a precious Eastern tapestry that will revive you in the middle of a hot day like a panacea. Of course one can improvise even with this classic dish: other herbs could be added, such as basil, dill or chopped arugula leaves.

3 OUNCES BULGAR (COARSE CRACKED WHEAT), PICKED OVER

7-OUNCE BUNCH OF FLAT-LEAVED PARSLEY, TRIMMED OF THICK STALKS

4 TABLESPOONS FINELY CHOPPED FRESH MINT

3-INCH PIECE OF CUCUMBER, PEELED AND DICED

3 SHALLOTS OR 1 MEDIUM RED ONION, DICED

3 SCALLIONS, FINELY CHOPPED

3 SMALL TOMATOES (ABOUT 7 OUNCES), SKINNED AND DICED

½ GREEN OR RED BELL PEPPER, DICED

FOR THE VINAIGRETTE:

JUICE OF 1½-2 LEMONS

3 TABLESPOONS OLIVE OIL

SALT AND FRESHLY GROUND BLACK PEPPER

SERVES 4-6

PREPARATION *about 30 minutes, plus 30 minutes' soaking and 30 minutes' marinating*

Calories per serving *153*
Total fat *High*
Saturated fat *Low*
Protein *Low*
Carbohydrate *Low*
Cholesterol *None*
Vitamins *A, B₁, B₃, Folate, C, E*
Minerals *Calcium, Potassium, Iron*

1 Rinse the bulgar and soak in hot water for 20 minutes. Drain well and roll it in a kitchen towel in order to get rid of excess moisture. Place it in a bowl.

2 Chop the parsley by hand, not too finely but not coarsely either—it should have some texture in it and should not be a puréed green mush. Add it to the bowl with all the other ingredients and mix everything together. Cover and chill lightly.

3 Half an hour before the salad is to be served, beat together the lemon juice with seasoning to taste. Then add the oil and beat until smooth.

4 Pour the dressing over the salad and toss well in order to coat everything in it. Taste and adjust the seasoning and add some more lemon juice if necessary.

5 Turn out on a platter to serve. The predominant color of the salad should be green.

Tabbouleh

MOROCCAN ORANGE, CARROT, OLIVE, AND ENDIVE SALAD

Golden oranges play a part at every Moroccan table, as part of a salad or as a garnish. Where there are oranges, there is also the warming aroma of cinnamon. In medieval Arab cooking, cinnamon was used in both savory and sweet dishes.

SERVES *4-6*

PREPARATION *15-20 minutes*

Calories per serving *80*
Total fat *Medium*
Saturated fat *Low*
Protein *Low*
Carbohydrate *High*
Cholesterol *None*
Vitamins *A, C, E, Folate*
Minerals *Iron, Potassium*

2 LARGE NAVEL ORANGES

6 OUNCES CARROTS

8-10 GREEN OLIVES, STONED AND QUARTERED

1 HEAD OF ENDIVE, TRIMMED

2 TABLESPOONS LIGHTLY TOASTED PINE NUTS

PINCH OF GROUND CINNAMON, TO GARNISH

FOR THE DRESSING:

2 TABLESPOONS LEMON JUICE

5-6 TABLESPOONS ORANGE JUICE

1 TABLESPOON CLEAR HONEY

2 TEASPOONS ORANGE FLOWER WATER

½ TEASPOON GROUND CINNAMON

1 Peel the oranges, removing as much white pith as you can. Slice the fruit horizontally into very thin rounds. Cover and chill.

2 Peel the carrots and pare into long shreds or grate them. Place the carrots and the quartered olives in a salad bowl.

3 Beat the dressing ingredients together until they are well blended. Reserving two tablespoonfuls, pour the dressing over the carrots and olives and toss until well coated.

4 Pull the endive leaves apart and arrange them with the orange slices on a round platter. Scatter the carrots over the salad and sprinkle the pine nuts and a pinch of cinnamon on top. Finally, drizzle the reserved dressing over the endive and serve.

ORANGE, OLIVE, AND ARUGULA SALAD

This unorthodox treatment of the exotic salads from Morocco has a sweet-and-sour taste.

SERVES *4*

PREPARATION *15-20 minutes, plus chilling*

Calories per serving *154*
Total fat *High*
Saturated fat *Low*
Protein *Low*
Carbohydrate *Low*
Cholesterol *None*
Vitamins *B₁, B₆, Folate, C, E*
Minerals *Potassium, Zinc*

3 LARGE ORANGES, PEELED AND THINLY SLICED

4 OUNCES BLACK OLIVES, HALVED AND PITTED

LARGE HANDFUL OF ARUGULA LEAVES OR WATERCRESS

3 TABLESPOONS FINELY CHOPPED PARSLEY OR CHERVIL

FOR THE VINAIGRETTE:

2 TABLESPOONS HAZELNUT OR WALNUT OIL

JUICE OF 1 SMALL ORANGE

1 TABLESPOON HONEY

SALT

1 Cut the orange slices into 4 and place in a bowl together with the remaining ingredients.

2 Whisk the vinaigrette ingredients together with salt to taste. Pour this into the salad and toss to coat everything in it.

3 Serve lightly chilled.

Moroccan Orange, Carrot, Olive and Endive Salad

Desserts

LEMON GRANITA

SERVES 6

PREPARATION 10
minutes

COOKING
5-6 minutes

FREEZING
4 hours, plus 30
minutes' ripening

Calories per serving 104
Total fat Low
Saturated fat Low
Protein Low
Carbohydrate High
Cholesterol None
Vitamins C
Minerals Potassium

These Roman water ices are at their best when made with very fresh fruit. Full of flavor, this simplest and most refreshing of desserts is wonderfully cleansing.

4 LEMONS, RINSED

HEAPING ½ CUP GRANULATED SUGAR

6 YOUNG MINT LEAVES, FINELY CHOPPED

1 Grate the rind of 2 of the lemons and set aside. Squeeze the juice from all of them.
2 Put 2½ cups of water in a pan with the sugar and lemon rind. Bring to a boil and simmer for 5-6 minutes. Remove from heat and add the mint and lemon juice. Let cool.
3 Empty the mixture into a suitable freezing tray and freeze for at least 6 hours. Take the tray out 2-3 times, at 2-hour intervals, to break the freezing contents up, mixing with a fork or turning it into a bowl and using an electric mixer. It should not freeze into a solid piece, but should have smaller particles.
4 Half an hour before it is to be served, transfer the granita to the refrigerator to allow it to ripen, i.e., make it softer and more pliable as well as more flavorful. Use a fork again to break up the ice if necessary before serving.

PEACH GRANITA

SERVES 6-8

PREPARATION 20
minutes

FREEZING
6 hours, plus 15
minutes' ripening

Calories per serving 73
Total fat Low
Saturated fat Low
Protein Low
Carbohydrate High
Cholesterol None
Vitamins C
Minerals Potassium

There is no more sumptuous finish to a meal on a hot summer evening, or indeed no better treat on a hot summer afternoon. Sometimes I also mix in 3-4 peeled fresh figs for a really exotic effect.

2 POUNDS RIPE PEACHES, PEELED AND PITTED

2 TABLESPOONS GRANULATED SUGAR OR HONEY

2 TABLESPOONS LEMON JUICE

3-4 FRESH FIGS, PEELED AND CHOPPED (OPTIONAL)

½ TEASPOON VANILLA EXTRACT

2 TABLESPOONS ROSE WATER

6-8 SMALL MINT LEAVES, TO DECORATE

1 If the peaches are ripe they are easy to peel, but if they are hard they have to be blanched quickly in a bowl of boiling water. Pit and slice each one into about 6 pieces.
2 Make a light syrup by boiling the sugar or honey in ⅔ cup of water for 3-4 minutes and then allow this to cool.
3 Place everything except the mint in a food processor and purée until smooth.
4 Pour the mixture into a container suitable for a freezer, cover, and freeze for 6 hours, taking it out every 2 hours to process again with the food processor or whisk in order to achieve a crystal-free texture.
5 Remove from the freezer about 15 minutes before it is to be served, otherwise it will be too solid. Serve in frozen glasses or bowls and decorate each with a couple of mint leaves.

Lemon Granita

BELILA
An Egyptian Breakfast

Belila *is an old Egyptian dessert that has recently become fashionable in smart Cairo hotels, but it has changed its identity and is now served as a healthy breakfast to the trend- and health-conscious. The dish consists of whole wheat grains that have been boiled and are then served with sweetened milk, nuts, and flavorings such as orange flower water or rose water. The wheat expands in volume and should not be overcooked or it will turn into a mass. So keep an eye on it toward the end.*

Many variations of the dish can be found around the Mediterranean. For instance, the Greek kolyva *offered at funerals and on All Souls Day is similar, but is served in a dry form without the milk and with a larger variety of nuts and spices. The same can be said about the Turkish* asure, *which has an enormous variety of ingredients—forty according to tradition—and includes rice and legumes, such as beans and chickpeas, as well as assorted dried fruits. This again is a kind of thick milky pudding and is supposed to be what Noah cooked with all the ingredients he had on the Ark. All these dishes seem related to the ancient Greek* panspermia, *a selection of wheat and nuts offered to the dead and the God of Hades.*

SERVES 6

PREPARATION *10 minutes, plus overnight soaking*

COOKING *about 1 hour*

Calories per serving *380*
Total fat *High*
Saturated fat *Low*
Protein *Low*
Carbohydrate *Low*
Cholesterol *10 mg*
Vitamins *B₁, B₃, B₁₂*
Minerals *Iron, Zinc, Iodine*

8 OUNCES WHOLE WHEAT GRAINS, SOAKED OVERNIGHT IN WATER
PINCH OF SALT
SCANT 2 CUPS MILK
1 TABLESPOON GRANULATED SUGAR

2 TABLESPOONS AROMATIC HONEY
4 TABLESPOONS ROSE WATER
SCANT 1 CUP FLAKED ALMONDS
SCANT 1 CUP PINE NUTS
SEEDS OF 1 POMEGRANATE (OPTIONAL)

1 Rinse the wheat, place in a pan, cover with water, add salt, and bring to a boil. Simmer gently, half-covered, for 35 minutes. Drain.
2 Bring the milk, sugar, and honey to a boil,

add the wheat, and simmer for about 10-15 minutes. Withdraw from the heat and mix in the rose water, nuts, and pomegranate seeds.
3 Offer with extra nuts, hot milk, and sugar.

TARTA DE NARANJA
Orange Custard

Oranges are the quintessential Mediterranean fruit. This Spanish dessert instantly evokes the Mediterranean in all its glory. Soft and delectable, it literally melts in the mouth.

SERVES 6

PREPARATION *15-20 minutes*

COOKING *45-50 minutes*

½ CUP GRANULATED SUGAR OR 3 TABLESPOONS OF AROMATIC HONEY
1¼ CUPS FRESH ORANGE JUICE (4-5 ORANGES), PIPS REMOVED BUT UNSTRAINED

4 EGG YOLKS, PLUS 1 WHOLE EGG
2 TABLESPOONS GROUND ALMONDS
3 TABLESPOONS ROSE WATER
2 TABLESPOONS COARSELY CHOPPED PISTACHIO NUTS

1 Preheat the oven to 325°F.

2 Mix the sugar or honey with ⅔ cup of water in a pan and boil gently for 4-5 minutes. Add the orange juice and simmer for about 2 minutes until slightly thickened. Let it cool for 10 minutes.

3 In the meantime, beat the eggs in a large bowl until pale and creamy and slowly add the hot orange mixture, beating continuously until smooth. Add the ground almonds and blend them well in. Finally, stir in the rose water and pour the mixture into a small soufflé dish or 6 individual ramekin dishes.

4 Bake in a bain-marie—placing the dish(es) in a larger dish filled with hot water that comes about halfway up the smaller dish(es)—for about 30-40 minutes until set.

5 Serve warm or lightly chilled. Sprinkle the custard with the pistachio nuts immediately before serving.

Calories per serving *180*

Total fat *High*

Saturated fat *Low*

Protein *Low*

Carbohydrate *Low*

Cholesterol *173 mg*

Vitamins *A, B₆, B₁₂, Folate*

Minerals *Calcium, Zinc, Iodine, Potassium*

HOSAF
Turkish Dried Fruit Dessert

Hosaf is an autumnal dessert common in Turkish homes. Dried fruit of high quality is therefore found in abundance in Turkish markets. A hosaf would normally be made up of a selection of fruits, including prunes. One can improvise, and alter the varieties of fruit suggested below according to availability. The addition of different nuts, like the pine nuts, makes the dish more luxurious, and the final sprinkling of scarlet pomegranate seeds adds an extra layer of flavor as well as a fairy-tale hint of the East.

¾ CUP PRUNES

¾ CUP DRIED FIGS

½ CUP DRIED APRICOTS

¼ CUP RAISINS

2 TABLESPOONS WHOLE SHELLED ALMONDS

1 TABLESPOON SUGAR

1 TABLESPOON HONEY

3 TABLESPOONS ROSE WATER

FOR DECORATION:

1 POMEGRANATE, PEELED AND DESEEDED

1 TABLESPOON PINE NUTS, TOASTED

SERVES *6*

PREPARATION *5-10 minutes*

COOKING *about 20 minutes, plus 4 hours' standing*

1 Several hours ahead of serving, or ideally the day before; rinse and drain the dried fruit. Boil the shelled almonds for 2-3 minutes, drain, and when they are cool enough to handle, skin them.

2 Mix the sugar and honey with 3¾ cups of water in a stainless steel pan and bring to the boil. Add the fruit and simmer for 15 minutes.

Add the almonds and simmer for 5 minutes more.

3 Stir in the rose water and leave the fruit to macerate in the syrup for at least 4 hours, or preferably overnight.

4 Serve at room temperature or warm up slightly. Scatter the pomegranate seeds and the pine nuts all over just before serving.

Calories per serving *221*

Total fat *Low*

Saturated fat *Low*

Protein *Low*

Carbohydrate *High*

Cholesterol *None*

Vitamins *B₂, B₆, E*

Minerals *Calcium, Potassium, Iron, Zinc*

BAKED PEACHES WITH PISTACHIO NUTS

1 HEAPING CUP SHELLED PISTACHIOS

2 MACAROONS OR AMARETTI BISCUITS

2 TABLESPOONS GROUND ALMONDS

2 TABLESPOONS CASTER SUGAR

½ TEASPOON GROUND CINNAMON

1 EGG YOLK

3 TABLESPOONS ORANGE BLOSSOM OR ROSE WATER

6 RIPE BUT FIRM PEACHES, HALVED AND PITTED

LIGHT FRESH FARMER CHEESE OR PLAIN LOW-FAT YOGURT, TO SERVE (OPTIONAL)

FOR THE SYRUP:

2-3 TABLESPOONS HONEY

2 CINNAMON STICKS

FEW STRIPS OF ORANGE PEEL

2 TABLESPOONS ORANGE BLOSSOM OR ROSE WATER

1 Preheat the oven to 350°F.
2 Coarsely chop the pistachio nuts and biscuits (this is quicker in a food processor). Empty into a bowl and mix into a paste with the almonds, sugar, cinnamon, egg yolk and orange blossom water or rose water.
3 Fill the cavity of each peach generously with this mixture, and arrange the fruit closely in a medium-sized baking dish.

4 Make the syrup: dissolve the honey in 1¼ cups of water over gentle heat, add the cinnamon and peel, and boil for 5-6 minutes until slightly thickened. Add the orange or rose water and pour around the peaches.
5 Bake for 15 minutes, until the peaches look soft without falling apart, basting occasionally. The peaches are delicious on their own, or served with fresh farmer cheese or yogurt.

SERVES 6

PREPARATION *about 20 minutes*

COOKING *about 20 minutes*

Calories per serving *218*
Total fat *High*
Saturated fat *Low*
Protein *Low*
Carbohydrate *Low*
Cholesterol *34 mg*
Vitamins B_1, B_3, B_{12}, C, E
Minerals *Calcium, Potassium, Iron, Zinc, Iodine,*

FIGS WITH MARSALA AND ORANGE

JUICE OF 2 ORANGES PLUS THE ZEST OF ONE, SLICED INTO THIN JULIENNE STRIPS

8-12 FIRM FRESH FIGS

⅔ CUP MARSALA OR A SWEET MUSCAT WINE SUCH AS SAMOS

2 TABLESPOONS AROMATIC HONEY

4 TABLESPOONS ORANGE FLOWER WATER OR ROSE WATER, OR 1 TEASPOON VANILLA EXTRACT

8 YOUNG MINT LEAVES

1 Combine the orange juice and Marsala or wine in a stainless steel saucepan. Bring to the boil and boil rapidly for 5 minutes to reduce it. Mix in the honey and the orange zest and simmer for 3-4 more minutes.
2 Place the figs in the pan and roll them around in the syrup over a gentle heat to

poach them for 2 minutes. They should not cook and soften but remain intact.
3 Off the heat, add the orange flower water, rose water, or vanilla and let it cool. Chill in the refrigerator for at least 1 hour.
4 Serve slightly chilled, coating the figs with their syrup. Decorate with mint leaves.

SERVES 4

PREPARATION *10 minutes*

COOKING *about 10 minutes, plus cooling and chilling*

Calories per serving *162*
Total fat *Medium*
Saturated fat *Medium*
Protein *Low*
Carbohydrate *Medium*
Cholesterol *10 mg*
Vitamins *C*
Minerals *Iron, Potassium*

Baked Peaches with Pistachio Nuts

PLUM OR PEACH CLAFOUTIS

This is one of the easiest, lightest and most versatile desserts to prepare. When we are at home on the Greek island of Alonnisos, as the summer proceeds I make it using different kinds of fruit.

In early July it is the small, bright yellow and honeyed local apricots. Our old friend Barba Nikos, who owns orchards of apricot trees, arrives early in the morning with quantities of aromatic fruit. Then the race is on to use them all. They make the most sumptuous jam; stewed apricots with Greek yogurt are served after lunch, and in the evenings the aroma of the freshly baked clafoutis spilling into the garden is irresistible.

Then the huge rosy-skinned peaches appear, to be followed by the juicy purple plums. Occasionally we pick small but very sweet blackberries from the hedges in the hillsides, and these are scattered over the other fruit in the clafoutis.

By the end of August, when our grapes start to ripen, I include a small bunch of these for good measure. The grapes have to be split in half and deseeded before they join the rest of the fruit.

Originally, of course, clafoutis was traditionally made with cherries and served during the cherry-picking season in the Limousin region of France.

SERVES *4-6*

PREPARATION
20 minutes

COOKING
about 50 minutes

Calories per serving *229*
Total fat *Medium*
Saturated fat *Medium*
Protein *Low*
Carbohydrate *Medium*
Cholesterol *150 mg*
Vitamins *A, B₂, B₃, B₆, B₁₂,*
Folate, C
Minerals *Calcium,*
Potassium, Iron, Iodine

½ TEASPOON SOFTENED BUTTER, FOR THE DISH

1¼ POUNDS PURPLE PLUMS OR PEACHES

2 TABLESPOONS GRANULATED SUGAR

FOR THE BATTER:

3 EGGS

4 TABLESPOONS GRANULATED SUGAR

1¼ CUPS MILK

½ CUP ALL-PURPOSE FLOUR, SIFTED WITH A PINCH OF SALT

1 TABLESPOON PURE VANILLA EXTRACT

LARGE PINCH OF GROUND CINNAMON

1 Preheat the oven to 375°F and butter a 10-inch flan dish or similar baking dish.

2 Slice the plums in half and pit them. If using peaches, first blanch them briefly in boiling water. Then skin and pit them, and cut them into quarters.

3 Arrange the fruit in the dish, skinned side down and closely packed in one layer. Sprinkle the sugar all over the top.

4 Make the batter: mix eggs, sugar, and milk together in the blender, add the flour, vanilla, and cinnamon, and blend until smooth.

5 Pour the batter mixture over the fruit and bake for about 50 minutes, until risen and golden on top. It will be studded with the colorful fruit, and the juices of the fruit will have made the dish meltingly soft and sweet .

6 Clafoutis is best served hot or warm.

Plum Clafoutis